HOME CELEBRATIONS

Home Celebrations

STUDIES IN AMERICAN PASTORAL LITURGY

by

LAWRENCE E. MOSER, S.J.

NEWMAN PRESS

Paramus, N.J./Toronto/New York

264.0274
mott

IMPRIMI POTEST:
Very Reverend Robert A. Mitchell, S.J.
Provincial, New York Province

July 13, 1970

NIHIL OBSTAT:
Msgr. Carroll Satterfield
Censor Librorum

IMPRIMATUR:
✝ Lawrence Cardinal Shehan
Archbishop of Baltimore

September 1, 1970

The Nihil Obstat and Imprimatur are official declarations that a book or pamphlet is free of doctrinal or moral error. No implication is contained therein that those who have granted the Nihil Obstat and Imprimatur agree with the contents, opinions or statements expressed.

Library of Congress   264.0274
Catalog Card Number: 72-133298

Published by Newman Press
Editorial Office: 304 W. 58th St., N.Y., N.Y. 10019
Business Office: Paramus, New Jersey 07652

Printed and bound in the
United States of America

Contents

THE SPIRIT IN LIFE

NEW BEGINNINGS

THE BEGINNING AND THE END

For my families—
all of them

Foreword

Central and critical to the life and health of the Church
community is the vitality of the family community. The sense
of God's presence is learned and experienced, first of
all, in the experience of love communicated and shared by
husband, wife, children and friends at home. Moreover, community life at home occurs not only within the family situation, but also in the shared experience and living of persons
who have come together to be part of each other's
lives, whether permanently or even in some more temporary
way. Sometimes these communities are composed of people
who share a common work; sometimes they are students, or
they belong to religious congregations; but always, if they
are authentic community, they belong in their freedom to
each other. They live in God's presence and in the presence
of each other. Their ritual and celebration gives expression
to their communal life while, at the same time, it draws them
closer together and brings new depths of insight and of life.
Community prayer, like the rest of their ritual activity,
celebrates their community-in-presence.

This volume is a presentation of celebrations for use at
home. Most of the emphasis in the celebrations themselves is
placed upon the needs of the family community situation, but
many of the liturgies will be suggestive or helpful in other
communities as well. Like *Eucharistic Liturgies,* the first
volume in the series of Studies in American Pastoral Liturgy, this collection is aimed very much at the contemporary
American religious scene, in the attempt to help crystallize
in community prayer the various elements of our religious
experience in this time of Spirit and newness. Like all rit-

1

uals and "rubrics," these should not be taken as the outside limits or finished products beyond which it is impossible to move. Rituals should not be the attempt to contain or control celebration; rather, they should be the jumping off place, the starting point, the inspiration for community prayer. It is our hope that families and other small-group communities will find some inspiration here for their prayer together.

John Gallen, S.J.
Center for Religion and Worship
Woodstock College

Preface

The liturgical celebrations that make up this book are tentative efforts, attempts at formulation and articulation—nothing more nor less. At their worst, they will net in word and gesture only the personal concerns and feelings of the author; at their best, they will hopefully enter into harmony with the often unspoken heart of God's people.

Here in the late twentieth century in America, I sense a kind of reticence, an uneasiness and shyness within the Christian family, about praying together. Why this should be so is not altogether clear. In one sense, it strikes roots in a certain modesty and reserve, in a reverence that hesitates to force intimacy or to put reins on another's freedom. Thus far, this hallmark of the American, and especially of the young American, is beautiful, healthy, grace-full. At least to some extent, however, this flight from expression may also be symptomatic of a widespread sense of insecurity and self-consciousness, of an apprehension that there is something vaguely "wrong" with family prayer. Further, it may be inspired by an image of *Church* as a place to which a person *goes* once a week for worship, rather than as that which we *are*—here and now, today and tomorrow, at all times and in all places, through every graced happening of our lives. God speaks here and now where two or three are gathered together, or he speaks not at all; and the first place where this gathering should take place is in the shared daily life of the Christian family. In short, the presupposition of this book is that one need not go looking for the Lord in whom we live. We will recognize him surely enough, if only our eyes are opened, in the breaking of the bread; we will speak of

3

him to one another, if only we are willing, in the communal family life of gift and concern, of openness and care, of word and touch. For this, the only life we know, has itself been touched by God and is patterned on his own life of love.

In writing a book such as this, a book in which ideas and words are skimmed from the surface of my own mind, I find without surprise that I am largely the sum of some thirty years of plagiarism. Echoes of poets, teachers, philosophers, spiritual writers, the many friends of my mind—all lend their unique flavors to these prayers. To list all of them, even those whose names I can consciously draw to the surface, would be interminable—if not impossible. I am all too aware, however, of their contribution. Suffice it to say, then, that I am deeply grateful to them, to each of them. While offering apologies for places where I fail to do them justice, I trust that whatever good may come of this book shall count as the small beginning of my thanks.

In its arrangement, this collection is quite arbitrary. Really, how does one set about "arranging" a life, capturing unceasing change in a system, or predicting the currents and flows by which one event will imperceptibly pass into another? The chosen format, however, does hint that each life, while ultimately a uniqueness of individual growth, looks in hope to the Lord who is and bestows meaning, looks to the one in whom beginning and end are gathered and crowned. Hence, the liturgical account of the institution of the eucharist is included—as the place where life is married to love, where life begins and ends its passage to Life.

Within the structure of each individual celebration, I hope that a good deal of scope is left for the play of creative ingenuity and for the unique contribution of every individual. Admittedly, though I myself most often picture the father of the family as the normal leader, there is no reason why this cannot be altered; the mother, a friend, or a sufficiently mature son or daughter could with equal effect conduct the celebration. Nor, for that matter, is the presence of an ordained minister a sure sign that it should be he who leads a celebration of some particular occasion. It may well be that the peculiar grace and presence that will give flesh to the skeleton meaning of the events here celebrated will perhaps not be as readily available to him as to a member of the family. Even if only the family is present, however, the readings should be parceled out among all, and should give rise to activity and to more than passive involvement on the part of each person. A celebration may never be a one-man happening—no matter who that man is, no matter what his gifts may be.

This book, then, explores the significance of some things that happen to us on the way, looks at some peaks in our ordinarily rather plain lives. All of them are times of celebration. As the effort of one relatively young man, however, to speak the center of what life says to us, they cannot be anything but incomplete in both the occasions selected and the meaning read out of them. Flexibility is the only answer to the problem of using these prayers. What can or cannot be of use must be decided on the basis of the uniqueness of each family—its customs, its patterns, its needs, and the rhythms of its love. Adaptation, subtraction, substitution, alteration—all are obviously necessary and strongly encouraged; this book is seed, not tree and leaf. And, I suppose, in prayer and in life, that flexibility, that willingness to grow, is something of what fatherhood and motherhood really mean: the grace of showing to children, to each of them in a uniquely delicate and lovely way, that love (and Love) is really alive in the family—and makes all the difference.

Lawrence E. Moser, S.J.

Beginnings

A Liturgy for
Birth

*At the dining table before the wife of the family returns
from the hospital; her customary place is left vacant, with a
candle burning before it. In the center of the table, an unlighted candle and, on a plate, a piece of bread. The father of
the family is celebrant, but depending upon the ages of the
other children, they, too, may do part of the reading which
will take the place of grace before the meal.*

*And God created man in the image of himself,
in the image of God he created him,
male and female he created them.
God blessed them, saying to them,
"Be fruitful, multiply, fill the earth . . ."
God saw all he had made,
and indeed it was very good.*

                    (Gn. 1: 27-28, 31)

*People brought little children to Jesus,
for him to lay his hands on them and say a prayer.
The disciples turned them away,
but Jesus said,
"Let the little children alone,
and do not stop them coming to me;
for it is to such as these
that the kingdom of heaven belongs."*

9

Then he laid his hands on them
and went on his way.

                    (Mt. 19: 13-15)

Father,
our Father,
it is our glory to be called your children,
and our grandeur to hand on to our children
    the gift of life
      and the touch of love.

    We thank you.

We thank you for all your gifts to us:
    for this food we are about to receive,
    for our home and family,
    and for N. (*name of newborn child*)
    whom you have given us today:
the flower of our love,
    warm and living,
    small but growing,
fragile and flickering as this candle,
but as nourishing to our love
    as bread to our bodies.

(*Here light the second candle*)

Light from light,
life from life,
love from love,
we give to one another what we are . . .
    and more.

Father,
send us your Spirit of love
   to clear our eyes of our smallness
   and of our lack of care for one another
   even here in this home.
Through him,
open our hearts to the need
   that you have made flesh in N. (*name of newborn child*)
and to the need of every man we meet.
For it is from the glitter of *our* eyes
   and the music of *our* voices,
from the warmth of *our* bodies
   and the softness of *our* hands,
that your son (daughter) N. (*name of newborn child*)
will come to learn
   how gentle is your love,
   and that Christ Jesus
   is your love for us.

(*The bread is broken into enough pieces for all present, and distributed*)

We remember him now,
as we prepare to eat this meal together,
for only broken for us as bread
could he teach us
   what love is really all about.

(*The bread is eaten*)

Children,
what we have done is a sign
   that speaks God's heart to us:
bread broken, chewed, swallowed,

gets inside us,
  becomes part of us;
love, too,
becomes a part of us,
  will grow and blossom,
    only if we are willing to hurt a little,
to be broken like that Lord
so that a little more happiness
  may rest in someone else's heart.

We have shared bread together.
Now let us share our love together,
and let us open our arms and our hearts
  to N. (*name of newborn child*)
  who will soon be with us
  at home.

(*Here exchange kisses, handshakes, etc.—whatever expressions of affection are customary within the family*)

Let us pray for one another,
  for Mother
  and for N. (*name of newborn child*),
as the Lord taught us.

(*Here recite the Lord's Prayer and eat dinner together*)

For the Birth
of a Grandchild

The liturgy is set at the table, perhaps before dinner, with flowers and two or three unlighted candles at the center of the group.

Rejoicing, let us come before the Lord;
filled with gladness,
    and in lightness of heart,
let us offer our thanks:

It is good to give thanks to the Lord God,
to pray in honor of your name, Most High,
to proclaim your love at daybreak
and your faithfulness all through the night . . .
I am happy, Lord God, at what you have done;
at your achievements I joyfully exclaim,
"Great are your achievements, Lord our God,
immensely deep are your thoughts!"
Planted in the house of the Lord,
the virtuous will flourish in the courts of our God,
still bearing fruit in old age,
still remaining fresh and green,
to proclaim that the Lord God is righteous,
my rock in whom no fault is to be found!
                    (*Ps. 92: 1-2, 4-5, 13-15*)

13

In the fullness of our time, Father,
  we come before you in great joy
    for the gift of our grandson (grandaughter)
      N. (*name of newborn child*).
In the flow of our years,
  it has too often seemed
    that we have cluttered our souls
      with useless and heavy baggage,
    that we slip more and more into loneliness
      with the passing of each day,
    that we have proven unequal
      to the work that you asked of us.

Yet, by your grace, Father, you still ask
  that we shoulder part of your work of creation:
    we form ourselves in the whirl and play of your world;
    never alone, we treasure the blessings
      of your loves in our hearts.
And now, at the very hour of ripeness and fruitfulness,
  you speak again today, Father—
    softly, gently, in a voice nourishing as rain
      to the earth.

You place in our hands
  the freshest of tasks:
    that of handing on to our grandchild
      only the best of what we are;
    that of replanting and tending once again,
      as we did in our own children,
        the tender seed of your love.

(Here light the candles)

In peace,
  let us hear the Word of God:

The Word was the true light
that enlightens all men;
and he was coming into the world.
He was in the world
that had its being through him,
and the world did not know him.
He came to his own domain
and his own people did not accept him.
But to all who did accept him
he gave power to become children of God,
to all who believe in the name of him
who was born not out of human stock
or urge of the flesh
or will of man
but of God himself.
The Word was made flesh,
he lived among us,
and we saw his glory,
the glory that is his as the only Son of the Father,
full of grace and truth.

                    (*Jn. 1: 9-14*)

Father, with the first breath of every child,
  with a voice crying in the wilderness,
    your Word comes again to his own
      and seeks acceptance.
As once our love was completed, made whole,
  in the birth of our own children,
    now again you make us new and enrich us

by the creation you and our children
have brought to light.
We learn of you still
from those whom we have taught.

Our Father, you call us now in your Spirit
to furnish the fuel
with which your son (daughter) N.,
our grandchild,
will warm his (her) life.

Whether the love of this child
will blaze into eternal life,
or flicker and die into embers,
may depend upon what we—
and no one else—
can provide.

Cast light upon us once again, Father,
as you have never ceased to do
through your Son.
May our own needs yield place
to those of your newborn son (daughter),
that from the fullness of your gifts to us
he (she) may receive full measure.

This we ask
to your glory,
in the name of your own Son Jesus,
and in the power of his Spirit.

(*Join hands, and pray the "Our Father"*)

On Moving into a
New Home

If only to preserve the composure of those involved, I see the celebration of this liturgy as taking place after some degree of order has been imposed upon the initial chaos of moving, and after perhaps a couple of days of rest. In other words, the celebration should be held soon after the family begins "living in a new home"—in contrast to merely "existing in a new house." During the initial blessing of the house, the family might move from room to room and, because of its rich symbolic value, sprinkle holy water in each of the rooms.

I heard a loud voice call from the throne,
"You see this city?
Here God lives among men.
He will make his home among them;
they shall be his people,
and he will be their God;
his name is God-with-them."

(*Rv. 21: 3*)

BLESSING OF THE HOME

(*To be carried out in each room, in terms that are associated with the "idea" of each room; the prayers for the individual rooms are merely offered by way of suggestion; at the close of each short prayer, the room may be blessed with holy water and with words similar to the following*)

17

Father, bless this room
  and fill it with your presence.
Let your peace rest
  upon those who make their home here
    and upon all who visit.
In the spirit of your Son,
  in the spirit of love,
    may all your children here find welcome.

KITCHEN

Our Father,
food shared between mother and child
  is your first gift,
    is the first taste we know of love.
May the preparation of food,
  the work of love done in this room,
    be a sign always
      that you dwell forever with us
        in the smallest things of your world.

                (*Blessing*)

BATH

Father, our Father,
water, too, is your gift to us:
  a sign of cleansing,
    a wonder of refreshment,
      the very possibility of life.
Keep us aware of our new life in you,
  and of your need of our cleansed hands
    to touch our world with love.

                (*Blessing*)

BEDROOMS

Father,
sleep is a source of strength in our lives.
Grant us all the deep peace with you
   that will let us rest soundly,
      so that we may return to your world each day
         awakened to your presence
         and alive to your call.

(*Blessing*)

LIVING ROOM

Father,
no room will have life
   unless touched by your love.
You have given us new life in your Spirit
   only that it may be shared,
      for each of us has a special love
         that only he can give.
If each of us does not burn,
   some darkness will be without your light.

(*Blessing*)

DINING AREA

Bless us and this room, Father,
   in ways known best to you,
      for only you fathom our deepest needs.
Through your grace,
   our need is more than filled in this home,
      in its nourishment,
      in its shelter.

Teach us to share, Father.
Teach us to share.

(Blessing)

Be compassionate as your Father is compassionate. Do not judge, and you will not be judged yourselves; do not condemn, and you will not be condemned yourselves; grant pardon, and you will be pardoned. Give, and there will be gifts for you: a full measure, pressed down, shaken together, and running over, will be poured into your lap; because the amount you measure out is the amount you will be given back.

(Lk. 6: 36-38)

LITURGY BEFORE DINNER

(*At the table before a meal, with three unlighted candles, and perhaps some flowers, in the center of the table*)

(*Light the first candle*)

Father of all men,
in the family life you have given to us,
   you have offered us yourself.

(*Light the second candle*)

Your Son lived with us
   in all the uncertainty and darkness of life,
     so that we might walk in your light.

(*Light the third candle*)

And he handed over to us his Spirit,
   as a light to guide our steps
      and as a brightness of heart
         to signal welcome to those
            who had found other doors closed.

Three candles shed one light;
   two of your children become one flesh;
      many foods eaten build one body.
Within each man, Father,
   you have planted a seed—
      the seed of your Son
         that grows no matter how deeply buried;
      the seed that will be a tree
         in whose branches
            all your children will come and rest.

Love calls us to the things of this world,
   and the many things of your world
      call us to the oneness and wonder of a home:
         a home such as you have given us
            for ourselves
            and for all your children.

Teach us to share, Father,
   as your own Son shared.
Teach us to share.
We ask this in his name
   and in his Spirit.

Amen.

For the Engagement
of a Son or Daughter

This celebration might be held either around the table or simply while the group sits together in the living room. I see no need to spell out the concrete signs of rejoicing that should accompany the prayer, for they will come, I think, quite naturally and from the heart. Who should be present is totally at the discretion of the families, but my own preference would lead toward at least both members of the couple and both pairs of parents. Unless the group thinks otherwise for their own reasons, it would seem fitting that the leader be the father of the son or daughter in whose home the gathering takes place.

Turning our minds and hearts to our Father,
   and thankful for his presence among us,
let us pray for N. and N. (*names of the couple*)
   whose engagement we celebrate today:

Out of his infinite glory, may the Father give you the power through his Spirit for your hidden self to grow strong, so that Christ may live in your hearts through faith, and then, planted in love and built on love, you will with all the saints have strength to grasp the breadth and the length, the height and the depth; until, knowing the love of Christ, which is beyond all knowledge, you are filled with the utter fullness of God.

(*Eph. 3: 16-21*)

22

Our Father, God of life and Lord of love,
   you have given each of us a life
      as a mountain to climb,
      a summit to be scaled,
         until we come to you,
            as men and women complete and whole,
         in the fullness of Christ Jesus.

Starting from different backgrounds,
   by winding paths,
      hand in hand with your other children,
we move upward,
   but never alone.
A fall is a fall, no matter whose,
   and a helping hand to one
      is stretched out in concern to all;
and over all, gently guiding,
   the Spirit who teaches the meaning of love.

But in wisdom past our grasp, Father,
   you have trusted us with special companions
      on our way:
         mothers and fathers from whose knees
            we take our first steps;
         brothers and sisters on whom we lean;
         friends who encourage us now and again
            on the way.

And today we especially rejoice
   because you have brought to the arms
      of our son (daughter) N. (*name of child*)
         the companion who will never leave
            his (her) side,
         and through whose presence

the road will take on new meaning,
even when steepest.

Six days later, Jesus took with him Peter and James and his brother John and led them up a high mountain where they could be alone. There in their presence he was transfigured: his face shone like the sun and his clothes became as white as the light. Suddenly Moses and Elijah appeared to them; they were talking with him. Then Peter spoke to Jesus. "Lord," he said, "it is wonderful for us to be here; if you wish, I will make three tents here, one for you, one for Moses and one for Elijah." He was still speaking when suddenly a bright cloud covered them with shadow, and from the cloud there came a voice which said, "This is my Son, the Beloved; he enjoys my favor. Listen to him." When they heard this, the disciples fell on their faces, overcome with fear. But Jesus came up and touched them. "Stand up," he said. "Do not be afraid." And when they raised their eyes they saw no one but only Jesus.

(*Mt. 17: 1-8*)

Father, it *is* wonderful for us to be here
    to share in these days
        the new light of happiness
            in the eyes of your children;
    to see with the new vision
        that looks with blessing upon all things
            and embraces their goodness.
For so you yourself looked, Father,
    in ages past,
        upon a world fresh from your hands.

Welcome N. and N. (*names of the couple*) into your love,
Father,
  and gather their love into yours,
    so that in the days of the breaking of the bread
      of soul and body
        which will surely come,
  they may stand straight
    in their faith in you
      and in one another.

(*Break a piece of bread and pass it around the table*)

Love remains whole when given away;
  life together becomes love when lived for another;
    only when eaten does bread build bodies and souls.

(*Consume the bread together*)

May your life together
  be ever lived in the light of Christ;
and may your upward road
  be ever in his footsteps
    and in the love of his Spirit.

(*Join hands for a moment of silent prayer*)

On the Departure
of a Son or Daughter

This celebration concerns itself with an occasion when a son or daughter leaves home for some rather extended period—going away to college, to military service, or something of the like. At the same time, however, younger children may feel with great intensity a much shorter separation (such as going away to camp for a summer), and an adapted version of the liturgy might prove of some help. Finally, I see no reason to withhold the celebration until the ultimate moment at the threshold. A more natural occasion would be at one of the last meals that the family shares as a unit—even if it be a number of days before the actual departure.

I lift my eyes to the mountains:
  Where is help to come from?
Help comes to me from the Lord God,
  who made heaven and earth.

No letting our footsteps slip!
  This guardian of yours, he does not doze!
The guardian of Israel
  does not doze or sleep.

The Lord God guards you, shades you;
  with the Lord at your right hand
sun cannot strike you down by day,
  nor moon at night.

26

The Lord guards you from harm,
  he guards your lives;
he guards you leaving, coming back,
  now and for always.

             (Ps. 121)

Our Father, you understand the hearts of all your children.
Look with love upon us as we come before you,
  not without concern,
    but with great joy,
      for N. (*name of child*)
        is about to leave our home.
As a gift to us,
  he (she) came into our family;
As a gift to all he (she) shall meet,
  we send him (her) in your care
    to your greater family,
    to all your children in our world.
We thank you, the giver,
  for the hours we have shared together,
    and for the times of still warmer joy—
      yet unknown,
        but sure to come.

Do not let your love be a pretense, but sincerely prefer good to evil. Love each other as much as brothers should, and have a profound respect for each other. Work for the Lord with untiring effort and with great earnestness of spirit. If you have hope, this will make you cheerful. Do not give up if trials come; and keep on praying. If any of the saints are in need you must share with them; and you should make hospitality your special care.

           (Rom. 12: 9-13)

But this, Father, is the time of action,
   the day of light for working,
      and not of troubled spirits.
Together, then, we pray now
   for your child,
      our son (daughter) N. (*name of child*).

(*These or similar petitions and responses may be used; more particular petitions may be added spontaneously by those present*)

That you keep your son (daughter) safe
   in all of his (her) travels . . . *Lord, we ask you to hear us.*

That you grant success, as you see fit,
   to him (her) in his (her) work . . .

That you keep alive in him (her) a great gentleness
   and a strong and active concern
   for each of your children . . .

That you nourish his (her) growth into full
   manhood (womanhood) in Christ . . .

That you strengthen him (her) in your love,
   and make firm the bonds of affection
   within this family . . .

That you bring him (her) home to us soon . . .

Our Father,
in the days when he walked among us

your own Son sent his friends forth
  to be about your work.
And though they were touched by the pain of separation,
  they found,
    to their surprise,
  that his love walked ever by their side.
Finally, on the night before his death,
  he broke the bread of his body.

(*Here break bread and pass it around to those present*)

He showed that where love makes his home
  parting becomes only a dream;
    that where hearts are one,
      distances are closed forever.

(*Here all consume the bread*)

Over the span of many years, Father,
  we have mingled what we are,
    and we have grown into one another.
In our hearts,
  let us carry one another with joy,
    and care for one another in love.
And let us be glad,
  in all things,
    for this day is the Lord's.

(*The mother and father here bless their child in these words,
or in others of their own choosing*)

May the Lord bless you and keep you.
May the Lord let his face shine on you
　and be gracious to you.
May the Lord uncover his face to you
　and bring you peace.
　　　　　　　　　　(*Nm. 6: 24-26*)

(*Exchange signs of affection*)

A Celebration on Retirement

This is a liturgy to be celebrated either within the family, or with the retiring person and a group of those closest to him or to her. Since thematically it is more taken up with the beginning of a new direction in life than with the concrete event of retirement, it need not coincide with the latter.

You are the light of the world.
A city built on a hill-top cannot be hidden.
No one lights a lamp to put it under a tub;
they put it on the lampstand
where it shines for everyone in the house.
In the same way your light must shine in the sight of men,
so that, seeing your good works,
they may give the praise to your Father in heaven.

(Mt. 5: 14-16)

Our Father, God of our lives,
we give you thanks for your gift of time,
   for this window of today
      that looks out on eternity,
   for the blessing of each moment
      in which the kingdom of heaven
         sinks its roots within us.
Our years, Father, have been full—
   rich with the harvest of life in togetherness,
   heavy with the fatigue and rewards of our work,
   graced with the pains of birth and growth.

31

But, above all, Father, they are completed years.
We can have no regrets,
>   but can only say at this moment of pause
>   >   that we would not have had them otherwise.

Time has made us what we are—
>   your children—
>   >   and we offer you our thanks.

In peace,
>   let us hear the Word of God:

So I say to you: Ask, and it will be given to you; search, and you will find; knock, and the door will be opened to you. For the one who asks always receives; the one who searches always finds; the one who knocks will always have the door opened to him. What father among you would hand his son a stone when he asked for bread? Or hand him a snake instead of a fish? Or hand him a scorpion if he asked for an egg? If you then, who are evil, know how to give your children what is good, how much more will the heavenly Father give the Holy Spirit to those who ask him!

> (*Lk. 11: 9-13*)

Father, you have indeed been good to us
>   in our days,
>   >   and we look forward to new and sturdy growth
>   >   >   as we enter upon this second spring
>   >   >   >   of our lives.

Help us in your Spirit, Father,
>   to recognize that your gifts to us

are not mere trifles for our own enjoyment,
but are the tools you have placed in our hands
to forge your world,
and the hearts of your children,
into the shapes of happiness.

Our years of maturity
still call us and challenge us to work:
now, as never before,
is the hour
when living example and the wisdom of experience
must be shared
with understanding,
gentleness,
and concern.

Each hour, minute, second, Father,
will never come again.
At long last, we have laid aside the burden of work
to set out on a new path,
to do what our hearts have long called us to.
And in your wisdom,
we retire not to an end, but to a beginning:
to the joy of a new and gentle work
made perfect in love.

Send over us the power of your Spirit, Father,
that this new step on our road to you
may be sure,
and taken in health of body and heart;
that our days may be those of a new creation
for ourselves,
and for each person
you have given into our care.

This we ask in the name of your Son,
　　risen and living,
and in the light of his Spirit,
　　leading and guiding,
　　　　today and all days.

(*Join hands, and pray the "Our Father"*)

For yours is the kingdom
　　and the power
　　　　and the glory,
　　　　　　now and forever.

Amen!

Life in the Spirit

On the Day of
Baptism

*This liturgy for the day of Baptism should, I think, precede
the actual celebration of the ritual; it is intended to set the
mental scene and to sharpen the awareness of the partici-
pants to their own part in what the community celebrates.
The setting is not of great importance, though appropriate-
ness would suggest that parents and godparents be present.
The structure breaks down into a series of three-part segments,
each intended, if possible, for three or more readers: the
first, a quotation from Scripture; the second, a rather gen-
eralized comment; the third, a comment more appropriate
to the occasion. After each segment, a short pause might be
inserted for meditation or for spontaneous reflections voiced
by those present.*

*Thus says the Lord God,
who made a way through the sea,
a path in the great waters. . . .
No need to recall the past,
no need to think about what was done before.
See, I am doing a new deed,
even now it comes to light; can you not see it?
Yes, I am making a road in the wilderness,
paths in the wilds.
The wild beasts will honor me . . .
because I am putting water in the wilderness
(rivers in the wild)
to give my chosen people drink.*

37

The people I have formed for myself
will sing my praises.
(Is. 43: 16, 18-21)

Father,
today we welcome into our family,
   into your family,
your son (daughter) N. (*name of the child*)
who will shortly be baptized
   into the new life of Christ.
Send upon each of us
   your Holy Spirit:
      that our lives may inspire this child
      in the strength of faith,
      in the joy of hope,
      in the reverence of love.

+

In this way we distinguish the children of God
from the children of the devil:
anybody not living a holy life
and not loving his brother
is no child of God's (*1 Jn. 3: 10*)

      But we, Father, are your children:
         born again of water and your Spirit
         in the promise of your Son's rising.
      Help us to grow in your Spirit:
         there is no standing still—
            the leaf grows green,
            or falls brown.

Today, Father,
your life takes root in N.
May it ever flourish and flower
to eternity.

✛

This is the message as you heard it
from the beginning:
that we are to love one another,
not to be like Cain, who belonged to the Evil One
and cut his brother's throat;
cut his brother's throat simply for this reason,
that his own life was evil
and his brother lived a good life. (1 Jn. 3: 11-12)

Within each of us, Father, is Cain:
the power to turn against you,
against our brothers;
to cause pain,
to enjoy another's suffering.
Help us to look ourselves in the face,
so that we may always taste our need for you
and for one another.

Lay Cain to rest, Father,
and end his wandering.
Bring the heart of this child
home to you:
for when you are found
nothing is lost,
all is gained.

✛

You must not be surprised, brothers,
when the world hates you;
we have passed out of death and into life,
and of this we can be sure
because we love our brothers. (1 Jn. 3: 13-14)

Father, if the world today really hated us,
perhaps that would be reason enough
for strength in faith.
Help us to grow in quiet and silence,
in the face of indifference,
when even faith may seem routine.

With your help, Father,
let our care of your son (daughter) N.
be the sign of faith:
for where there is care,
there indifference and unbelief vanish,
and you are found again
in the midst of your people.

✝

If you refuse to love, you must remain dead;
to hate your brother is to be a murderer,
and murderers, as you know,
do not have eternal life in them. (1 Jn. 3: 15)

Your Spirit, Father, is Love itself,
is your gift of meaning to life.
We are questions, Lord,
each to each—
only your Spirit is an answer.

Open our hearts to the question
you ask, Lord,
in your child N.
May our answer be ever your answer:
an invitation to come in,
and to rest.

+

This has taught us love—
that he gave up his life for us;
and we, too, ought to give up our lives
for our brothers. (1 Jn. 3: 16) ˙

Touch our eyes, Father,
sharpen our vision to the signs
your world speaks to us:
water poured out, cleansing;
bread broken and eaten,
grapes crushed, nourishment;
a man dying for another,
eternal life.

We shall not be called upon
to die for your child N.
We shall be asked often
to lay down comfort and convenience,
to put away likes and dislikes,
so that he (she) may meet you in us.
Awaken your strength in us,
for that day,
for every day.

+

If a man who was rich enough in this world's goods
saw that one of his brothers was in need,
but closed his heart to him,
how could the love of God
be living in him? (1 Jn. 3: 17)

Father, is there any of our brothers,
    any of your children,
who is not in need?
You know what need we have,
    more than enough;
and our greatest need is a share
    in your eyes and in your heart:
        open, ready to be broken.

At our expense, Lord,
allow the little children
    to come to us,
    and to teach us;
for it is to them,
    and to those like them,
        that your kingdom belongs.

+

My children,
our love is not to be just words or mere talk,
but something real and active;
only by this can we be certain
that we are children of the truth. (1 Jn. 3: 18-19)

In many ways, Father,
we shall never be certain,
    but we shall know
    that we have tried.

Help us to live with the question of Love,
   to love now with the knowledge
   that your greater Love,
      even while in our midst,
   shall return
   to measure our little loves
      against himself.

Let us pray together for N.
in the words the Lord has taught us:

(Recite the "Our Father," with hands joined)

On the Day of
First Communion

This liturgy may be held either before or after the Eucharist at which the First Communion takes place; it might equally well serve as grace before dinner on that day. In either case, it is concerned with bread and wine, and with the giving of thanks for the kind of world that has been given to us. It is a celebration and a thanksgiving: because at the heart of the smallest, the greatest has made a home; because there is nothing we know that is what it seems—all is far, far more. The questions concerning bread and wine might be asked by the child whose First Communion is celebrated, and the answers may have to be rewritten accordingly.

Look, I am standing at the door, knocking.
If one of you hears me calling and opens the door,
I will come in to share his meal,
side by side with him.

(Rv. 3: 19-20)

My brothers and sisters,
my children,
today we celebrate the Eucharist:
   we pause to do
      what a person first does with any gift.
We say thank you.

44

We thank you, Father,
    because you have given us this earth
        as our only path to yourself;
    because you have made the things of your world
        the instruments from which our hands
            may draw the music
                of your Word to us.
Help us, Father,
that we may help your creation sing.

That very same day, two of them were on their way to a village called Emmaus, seven miles from Jerusalem, and they were talking together about all that had happened. Now as they talked this over, Jesus himself came up and walked by their side; but something prevented them from recognizing him. He said to them, "What matters are you discussing as you walk along?" They stopped short, their faces downcast.

Then one of them, called Cleopas, answered him, "You must be the only person staying in Jerusalem who does not know the things that have been happening there these last few days." "What things?" he asked. "All about Jesus of Nazareth," they answered, "who proved he was a great prophet by the things he said and did in the sight of God and of the whole people; and how our chief priests and our leaders handed him over to be sentenced to death, and had him crucified. Our own hope had been that he would be the one to set Israel free. And this is not all: two whole days have gone by since it all happened; and some women from our group have astounded us: they went to the tomb in the early morning, and when they did not find the body, they came back to tell us they had seen a vision of angels who declared he was alive. Some of our friends went to the tomb and found everything exactly as the women had reported, but of him they saw nothing."

*Then he said to them, "You foolish men! So slow to believe
the full message of the prophets! Was it not ordained that the
Christ should suffer and so enter into his glory?" Then, starting with Moses and going through all the prophets, he explained to them the passages throughout the scriptures that
were about himself.*

*When they drew near to the village to which they were go-
ing, he made as if to go on; but they pressed him to stay with
them. "It is nearly evening," they said, "and the day is almost
over." So he went in to stay with them. Now while he was
with them at table, he took the bread and said the blessing;
then he broke it and handed it to them. And their eyes were
opened and they recognized him; but he had vanished from
their sight. Then they said to each other, "Did not our hearts
burn within us as he talked to us on the road and explained
the scriptures to us?"*

(*Lk. 24: 13-32*)

What is bread?

> Father, our Father,
>   and Father of all men,
> we are so content to eat bread
>   and to forget its story.
> We are slow to make the effort,
>   slow to see.

> Bread:
>   the work of many hands,
>   the death of many small grains of wheat,
>   becomes the body of your Son.
> The body of your Son,

broken and chewed and eaten,
   is flesh of our flesh.

But we cannot take God's bread
   to ourselves
until we have seen Christ our brother
   sitting next to us
   at the table.

(*Here break a piece of bread*)

Bread shared
   invites every man
      to come in and rest.

What is wine?

Many grapes
   grown to ripeness,
   crushed and broken,
      that they may carry joy to man.
We hesitate to drink wine alone:
   it livens our feasts,
   breaks down walls between men,
   lets them taste the foolishness of generosity
      and the wisdom of trust.

Why are these things so?

All of this is a sign:
   that we may know that your Word
      comes not from heaven,
         but from the gifts of this world;

that we may not go about with eyes raised to heaven,
　　when the Lord lives with us
　　　in the flesh;
that we may touch the goodness of a God
　　who dares to differ
　　　from what we should like to expect.

Let us share bread broken
　　and offer this cup
　　　one to another.

(*Here share bread and wine*)

Every Communion is a First Communion
　　such as we celebrate today:
　　　for we possess you, Lord,
　　　　as a promise,
　　　　as a call,
　　　　as a challenge—
　　　　　ever the same,
　　　　　ever new and unrecognized.

We must heal your world,
　　Father,
but like all your children,
　　we must take our first faltering steps
　　　from where we are.

Together,
let us join hands
　　in peace.

(*Hold hands for a moment of silent prayer*)

A Liturgy for Maturity

This liturgy might take place at the dinner table either before or after a Confirmation ceremony—though the needs of a particular family might dictate that the liturgy not coincide with the reception of the sacrament: the age of maturity is an unpredictable thing. In any case, the table should be set festively and, most especially, there should be flowers on it: flowers, plants from about the house, all kinds of growing things. For the young man or young lady, the celebration is seen as a promise and an instruction; for the older people it is a reminder and an invitation.

You will know that I am in the midst of Israel,
that I am the Lord your God, with none to equal me.
My people will not be disappointed any more.
After this I will pour out my Spirit on all mankind.
Your sons and daughters shall prophesy,
your old men shall dream dreams,
and your young men see visions.

(Jl. 2: 27; 3: 1)

My brothers and sisters,
the Lord God says:

> *Think of the flowers growing in the fields;*
> *they never have to work or spin;*

> *yet I assure you that not even Soloman*
>   *in all his regalia*
>   *was robed like one of these.*
>   *Now if that is how God clothes the grass in the field*
>   *which is there today*
>   *and thrown into the furnace tomorrow,*
>   *will he not much more look after you,*
>   *you men of little faith?*

(Mt. 6: 28-30)

Our Father, we give you our thanks
    because we set this day aside
        to celebrate a new beginning
            for your son (daughter) N.
Through the love of his (her) parents,
    you have shared with him (her) life;
        in his (her) sharing of life with others,
            you have touched him (her) with your Spirit
                and nourished his (her) growth.

(*The following is to be read by the young man or young
woman*)

Father, you have given me a body like your Son's,
    a body with which I can make visible
        the seed of love you have planted within me
            and my restless need to share myself
                with your other children.
You call me in your world, Father,
    toward a body and soul other than my own,
        and I thank you.

My body, Father, is a word,
　is your Word,
　　is a question.
And now, as I grow, that question,
　the beginning of your wish to touch another in me,
　　cries for an answer.
Your Spirit of love,
　within me and outside me in your children,
　　my brothers and sisters,
　　　breathes in our world.

Speak your Word, Father, in me.
　Do not leave my love unused,
　　or let me twist it to my own ends.

(*The leader offers the following prayer*)

Father, you have given us one life,
　and at the center of that life
　　the love which is Christ.
　　　Toward him and in him we grow.
Our choice, your choice, is the foolhardy glory of the flower:
　to live with intensity and beauty,
　　even as we move toward our home in you;
　to take a leap into the uncertainties of love,
　　rather than live locked in loneliness.
Like the water of a fountain,
　we trace beauty only as we give ourselves away.

We pray now for your son (daughter) N.
　who today is graced
　　with a new gift of your Spirit.

(Join hands in prayer; the following to be said by the father of the young man or woman)

Father, pour out your Spirit
    upon my son (daughter) N.
        and make him (her) strong in your love:
            alive with concern,
            warm with gentle strength,
            and openhearted in sharing.
His (her) years may be few or many,
    as you know best,
        but let them be full years:
            years of firm faith,
            years of unfailing hope in you
                and in your children,
            years of responsible and unshakable love.
This we ask, Father, in the name of your Son,
    and in the grace of his Spirit within us,
        living and guiding,
            today and forever.

Amen.

(Exchange congratulations)

A Family Service of Forgiveness

This communal liturgy looks forward to the first reception of the sacrament of Penance, whenever that may occur. Therefore it contains a brief examination of conscience. It is most important that the content of the latter be altered by the parents on the basis of what they see of the maturity and needs of their own child. Further, one must continually keep in mind that Penance is a sign of forgiveness and acceptance, not a traumatic taste of guilt and self-punishment. Just as the examination of conscience and the act of contrition are communal, therefore, if circumstances permit, it would be fitting and supportive for the child that when the occasion arises the whole family also receive the sacrament together.

Since in Jesus, the Son of God,
we have the supreme high priest
who has gone through to the highest heaven,
we must never let go of the faith that we have professed.
For it is not as if we had a high priest
who was incapable of feeling our weaknesses with us;
but we have one who has been tempted
in every way that we are,
though he is without sin.
Let us be confident, then, in approaching the throne of grace,
that we shall have mercy from him
and find grace when we are in need of help.

(Heb. 4: 14-16)

Our Father,
we place ourselves before you
   knowing well that we have all done wrong:
      in the evil that we have done,
      and in the good that we have not troubled to do.
You ask us only to do to your other children,
   to our brothers and sisters,
      what we would like them to do to us;
        but we, small and selfish,
          do to them and for them
            only what gets us what we like.
Together now,
   let us look at ourselves as we are
   and ask God's help to be better.

(These or similar reflections and responses may be used in an examination of conscience)

For failing to remember that we ourselves,
   and all we have, are your gifts to us . . . *Lord, have mercy.*

For failing to pray because we had other things
   to do that seemed more important . . .

For failing to respect our parents and all
   others whose love makes them care about us . . .

For being angry and deliberately trying to hurt
   others who are also your children . . .

For spending too much time looking after our bodies,
   or for not being careful enough with them . . .

For taking what does not belong to us,
  or for being tight-fisted and selfish
  with what we have . . .

For speaking unkindly of others or without care
  for their feelings, and for using the gift of
    speech to cause pain . . .

For being jealous of others, and unthankful for
  the many gifts you have given each of us . . .

For being afraid to stand up
  for what we know is right . . .

For not going out of our way to help others
  because we might be hurt
    or because it was too much trouble . . .

For not using your many gifts to bring happiness
  into any lives except our own . . .

(*Pause here for a minute or two of reflection and prayer*)

Jesus also said, "A man had two sons. The younger said to his father, 'Father, let me have the share of the estate that would come to me.' So the father divided the property between them. A few days later, the younger son got together everything he had and left for a distant country where he wasted his money on a life of fun and games.

"When he had spent it all, the country experienced a severe shortage of food, and now he began to feel the pinch of want, so he hired himself out to one of the local people who put

him on his farm to feed the pigs. And he would willingly have filled his belly with the food the pigs were eating but no one offered him anything. Then he came to his senses and said, 'How many of my father's paid servants have more food than they want, and here I am dying of hunger! I will leave this place and go to my father and say: Father, I have sinned against heaven and against you; I no longer deserve to be called your son; treat me as one of your paid servants.' So he left the place and went back to his father.

"While he was still a long way off, his father saw him and felt sorry for him. He ran to the boy, took him in his arms and kissed him tenderly. Then his son said, 'Father, I have sinned against heaven and against you. I no longer deserve to be called your son.' But the father said to his servants, 'Quick! Bring out the best clothes and put them on him; put a ring on his finger and new shoes on his feet. Bring the food we have been saving for a special occasion and get it ready; we are going to have a feast, a celebration, because this son of mine was dead and has come back to life; he was lost and is found.' And they began to celebrate."

(*Lk. 15: 11-24*)

(*Lk. 7: 36-50 might also be used in the above liturgy*)

Father, we come before you
   knowing that we have fallen,
      and you tell us to stand up and walk.
We cannot change the past,
   for what is done, is done;
      but today and tomorrow are your call to us.
Support us, Father, and hold us up
   with a full sense of how forgiving you are,

so that we may avoid the final wrong
    of refusing to take you at your Word,
    of wanting to stay on the ground after a fall.

Your Word of forgiveness to us, Father,
  is terribly serious:
    it took sweat, and nails, and blood—
    the body and life of your own Son—
    for you to say to each of us:
    "I forgive you, and I love you."
For this we are ever filled with thanks,
  and will do our best
    to make our thanks real in the way we live
    in days to come.

(*Join hands and recite together the "Act of Contrition"*)

A Liturgy during
Illness

*Whether this liturgy should or should not be celebrated in
the presence of the person who is ill will have to be judged
in accordance with his or her physical and emotional condi-
tion. In either case, the liturgy is more directed toward those
who are well, toward mobilizing in them a living and affective
concern and understanding.*

Listen to me, Lord, and answer me,
poor and needy as I am;
keep my soul: I am your devoted one;
save your servant who trusts in you.

You are my God; take pity on me, Lord.
I call upon you all day long;
give your servant reason to rejoice,
for to you, Lord, I lift my soul.

Lord, you are good and forgiving,
most loving to all who call to you;
Lord God, hear my prayer,
listen to me as I plead.

Lord, in trouble I call upon you,
and you answer my prayer;

there is no God to compare with you,
no achievement to compare with yours.

Lord God, you are always kind and tender-hearted,
slow to anger, always loving, always loyal;
turn to me and pity me.
(Ps. 86: 1-8, 15-16)

Remembering that the Lord is with us
   wherever we are,
     let us lay open our hearts
      in his presence:

(*Pause*)

Our Father,
we come to you in a moment of sickness
   when N. (*name of person who is ill*)
     cannot be here with us.
Our hearts are not at rest, Father,
   and the rhythm of our lives
     has been broken.
Yet we are sure that you desire nothing
   but what is best for us,
     and that our needs move your heart
      as the heart of a Father.

Then Jesus withdrew from the disciples, about a stone's throw
away, and knelt down and prayed. "Father," he said, "if you are
willing, take this cup away from me. Nevertheless, let your
will be done, not mine." Then an angel appeared to him, com-
ing from heaven to give him strength. In his anguish he prayed

even more earnestly, and his sweat fell to the ground like
great drops of blood.

(Lk. 22: 41-44)

Our Father,
in his night in the garden,
   Jesus Christ, your Son and our brother,
      shouldered the weight of human pain and suffering.
In him we see
   that even our frailty is a gift:
      to welcome it as your will
         cannot ever be easy,
      but to do so
         will grace it with meaning.
Our failure is to try to suffer alone,
   and our glory to carry the pain of another.

Stir up in us, Father, during these days,
   a keen concern
      for N. (*name of the person who is ill*),
         that we may help him (her)
           with ready understanding,
           with loving and working hands.
Let our love take flesh
   in the quiet and peace
      that will speed his (her) recovery.
And touch N. (*name of person who is ill*)
   with your peace, too, Father—
      with that calm of soul
         that will smooth his (her) path
           to health and strength.

This we ask together, Father—
   N. and N. (*names of all those present*)—
      if it be your will.

Hear us,
  as you listened to your Son,
    Christ Jesus,
      in whose words we pray.

(*Join hands, and pray together the "Our Father"*)

A Liturgy for
Advent

This liturgy may be celebrated anywhere in the home and may be used in conjunction with an Advent wreath: a wreath of greens lying on a table with four candles (three purple and one white) rising from it. The first candle is lighted on the first Sunday of Advent, and an additional candle is lighted at the beginning of each of the subsequent weeks.

I wait for the Lord, my soul waits for him.
  I rely on his promise;
  my soul relies on the Lord
  more than a watchman on the coming of dawn.
Let Israel rely on the Lord
  as much as the watchman on the dawn!
For it is with the Lord that mercy is to be found,
  and a generous redemption;
  it is he who redeems Israel
  from all their sins.

(*Ps. 130: 5-8*)

Father,
we turn our minds and hearts to you
  because we are waiting for your coming.
Our world is filled with the sounds of poverty,
  with the cries of your hungry children.
Casting the fire of war upon the earth,

we, despite ourselves,
    do battle against the fire of your Spirit.
We wait again for your coming,
  for the new birth of your Son,
    yet we lack the bold confidence
      of facing your stillness
        amid the clatter of our concerns.

In the countryside close by there were shepherds who lived in the fields and took it in turns to watch their flocks during the night. The angel of the Lord appeared to them and the glory of the Lord shone round them. They were terrified, but the angel said, "Do not be afraid. Listen, I bring you news of great joy, a joy to be shared by the whole people. Today in the town of David a savior has been born to you; he is Christ the Lord."

(Lk. 2: 8-11)

Father,
you have already come near to us
  in the gift of Christ Jesus,
    your Son and our brother.
Otherwise we would not be waiting,
  otherwise we would not be looking for the birth of love
    in our world.
The light we await is already shining,
  the source of the pain of our longing,
  the small voice
    which will not let us rest content
      with what we are.

For when peaceful silence lay over all
and night had run the half of her swift course,
down from the heavens, from the royal throne,
leapt your all-powerful Word.

(Wis. 18: 14-15)

The silence is broken
　once for all:
　　you have named us your sons,
　　　christened us,
　　and have asked only that we act as such
　　　toward you,
　　　　and toward our brothers.

Shatter our narrowness, Father,
　and awaken our ears
　　to the sounds of silence—
　　　for the silence is filled with many voices.
We wait for you
　because we know only too well
　　that you are far more
　　　than anything our minds have grasped or fashioned.
But we wait in the knowledge
　that you have already given yourself,
　and that you shall never go back on your Word.

We shall kindle the lights of Christmas, Father,
　the lights of our rejoicing.
Grace them, and make them a sign
　of warmth and of acceptance stronger than words,
　　of fire that wishes to spread,
　　　of a light that darkness will never grasp.

In a burning bush
    you spoke to Moses, our father in faith;
in a pillar of fire
    you led your children out of captivity
        into the freedom of your love;
in the fire of your Spirit
    speak to us
        and cast flame upon the dry places of our hearts.
Make us today your Church,
    the beacon of your presence in the world.
This we ask in the name of Christ Jesus,
    born today and everyday
        until the end of time.

Amen.

A Celebration for
Christmas Eve

In this liturgy, perhaps of all those in the book, nothing is so much required as the gifts of spontaneity and free-wheeling joy: the slightest stilting or forcing of Christmas Eve invites ruin. On the premise of this book, however, it becomes difficult to say just where liturgy begins or ends—so that there is no kind of activity that cannot fall gracefully within its pale, especially, I think, the marvelously unpredictable doings of children.

It might be well, therefore, except for some brief symbolic segment of formal prayer, to make this celebration as utterly unstructured as possible, to turn the prayers into scattered significant and simple comments of the parents to their children, while engaged in the actual work of the evening. I somehow feel that this would be far more effective, and affective, than what is presented here. Though cast within a somewhat rigid form, then, these prayers are more intended to furnish the parents a point of departure than for anything else.

What can or cannot be done will, of course, depend upon the ages of the children, their degree of maturity, the state of their minds regarding Santa Claus, and so forth. Once Santa has had his due, however, I would like to see each child contribute something to the general feast: a little girl, for example, "helping" with some baking; a boy spending some time in making decorations or ornaments. This is their offertory, and imagination can run riot; often, they will be more inventive than adults.

(Sing the first verse of "O Come, All Ye Faithful")

Shout to the Lord, all the earth,
serve the Lord with gladness,
come before him with songs of joy!
Know that he, the Lord, is God;
he made us and we belong to him;
we are his people, the flock he cares for.

Walk through his house giving thanks;
enter his rooms praising him;
give thanks to him, bless his name!

Yes, the Lord God is good;
his love has no end;
he is faithful from age to age.

                                    (Ps. 100)

(The second verse of the carol is sung here)

TRIMMING THE TREE

(Even if the tree lights must be on during decoration, they should be turned off afterward and relighted later in the evening)

Our Father,
we come to you in gladness—
    N. and N. *(names of all those present)*—
on this night when we celebrate
    your Son's quiet gift of himself
        to our world,
We bring this tree, a living sign of your Fatherhood,

into our home;
    among its branches,
        we weave brightness and light;
            let it flow with rivers of tinsel.
We drape its limbs with gifts we have made,
    and with joy and thanks,
        rather than, as the story goes,
            trying to take their fruit from them by force.
Remember us this night, Father,
    remember all the days of our lives
        when the open giving of Christmas
            was most bright in us.
In the Spirit of your Son,
    let days lived for others
        shine ever more clearly in our lives.

(*Proceed to trim the tree*)

ARRANGING THE CRECHE

(*Once the arrangement is in final order, then, with all present,
and with just a single candle burning, the figure of Christ
should be placed in its midst; before beginning work, the
family might sing "O Little Town of Bethlehem"*)

Father,
your Son came to his own as a baby—
    to the poor and uneducated,
    to those with uncluttered hearts,
        to those who had the sight to see
        just how much they needed him.
And again and again each day, this day,
    he comes to us

in the poor who are still with us,
in the question of each man
who is cold and needy in some corner of his heart,
if not in appearance.

(Have just a single candle burning during the following read-ing)

While Mary and Joseph were at Bethlehem, the time came for her to have her child, and she gave birth to a son, her first-born. She wrapped him in swaddling clothes, and laid him in a manger because there was no room for them at the inn. In the countryside close by there were shepherds who lived in the fields and took turns watching their flocks during the night. The angel of the Lord appeared to them and the glory of the Lord was bright all around them. They were terrified, but the angel said, "Do not be afraid. Listen, I bring you news of great joy, a joy to be shared by the whole people. Today in the town of David a savior has been born to you; he is Christ the Lord. And here is a sign for you: you will find a baby wrapped in swaddling clothes and lying in a manger." And suddenly with the angel there was a great crowd of the heavenly host, praising God and singing:

*"Glory to God in the highest heaven,
and peace to men who enjoy his favor."*

Now when the angels had gone from them into heaven, the shepherds said to one another, "Let us go to Bethlehem and see this thing that has happened which the Lord has made known to us." So they hurried away and found Mary and Joseph, and the baby lying in the manger.

(Lk. 2: 6-16)

The Lord Jesus is come;
   let us lift up our voices!

(Place the figure in the crèche, light the tree again, and sing something like "Silent Night" or "Hark, the Herald Angels Sing")

THE EXCHANGE OF GIFTS

Father, you gave us your own Son
   to show us that giving has no meaning
      unless we give ourselves and our love
         together with the gift.
As we share these presents with one another,
   help us to learn
      how to give not just what we have, but what we are;
      how to be thankful for what we receive;
      how to make every day a Christmas
         for one or another of your children.

(Sing "Joy to the World," exchange gifts, and, perhaps, eat something together)

A Liturgy for
Ash Wednesday

*A liturgy such as this is intended as a simple meditative re-
minder of who and what we are—the very thing we look
upon least often in the welter of our efforts to "do" things.
During the invocation, in keeping with the symbolism of the
day, the palms from the previous year might be burned in the
midst of the group. And following the liturgy, the family
might share a meal of modest size, but a meal somehow
noticeably less in quality or quantity than what is normal
fare for the persons involved.*

*Not by us, Lord our God, not by us;
by you alone is glory deserved,
by your love and your faithfulness!
Do the pagans ask, "Where is their God?"*

*Ours is the God whose will is sovereign
in the heavens and on earth,
whereas their idols, in silver and gold,
products of human skill,*

*have mouths but never speak,
eyes, but never see,
ears, but never hear,
noses, but never smell,*

*hands, but never touch,
feet, but never walk,*

and not a sound from their throats.
Their makers will end up like them,
and so will anyone who relies on them.

House of Israel, rely on the Lord God,
on him, our help and shield!

                (*Ps. 115: 1-9*)

Recalling that you are ever present among us, Lord,
    we admit our smallness and lack of care,
        and we ask your help:

(*These or similar petitions and responses may be used*)

That our desires, and even our desire to do good,
    may never become our false gods . . . *Hear us, Father.*

That we may train our souls and bodies
    as tools for your work,
        and not because of our own pride . . .

That we may love every thing and each thing
    without grasping it in greed and selfishness . . .

That our worship of you may be in spirit and in truth,
    and not merely an outward show . . .

That we may be strong to suffer the simple pain
    of living in love . . .

That we may be graced with the wisdom of hearing
    your voice in all your children . . .

But when the kindness and love of God our savior for man-kind were revealed, it was not because he was concerned with any righteous actions we might have done ourselves; it was for no reason except his own compassion that he saved us, by means of the cleansing water of rebirth and by renewing us with the Holy Spirit which he has so generously poured over us through Jesus Christ our savior. He did this so that we should be justified by his grace, to become heirs looking forward to inheriting eternal life. This is doctrine that you can rely on.

(*Tit. 3: 4-8*)

Father, your gifts to us have been gracious—
   born from your undying care,
     unearned by our actions,
      and passing every expectation.
Preserve us during these days
   from the idolatry of mistaking
     the gift for the giver:
      from trying to still our longing
       with what is passing;
      from setting our hopes
       upon what rests on sand.

Where you could have given only a world,
   from your hands came instead
     the possibility of a home.
Where we had earned your anger,
   you spoke gently in the gift of your Son,
     so that our narrow eyes
      might see that you are Love.
And still we say that we love you in your heaven,
   while we leave the hearts of your children on earth
     cold and bare.

Only a house uninhabited
is without dust.

Ash Wednesday, Father, is your reminder.
We are dust . . .
we are your children,
the glory of your creation.
We shall return to dust . . .
we shall return to your arms,
and receive the welcome of sons.
But in the meantime, with your help,
like the dust of this world,
we shall settle everywhere,
and make your presence felt.
Unpeopled hearts, by your grace,
shall become homes.

The journey to heaven, Lord,
begins with the dust of Ash Wednesday:
with dust set aside as a reminder,
but also with the dust of bus and subway,
of street and avenue.
We are a people on the move,
and what we do, or do not do,
to the least of our fellow travelers,
we do to you.
Love that to come alive
must look further than the person at its elbow
is not your love.
By your design, Father,
we are no nearer to you
than we are to our neighbor—
to any man, to *this* man.

Father, we cannot be good alone,
    for only when we are loved
        does our strength prove equal to the task.
Share your love with us during these days,
    as we look forward to the new life of Easter,
        so that they may be days
            not of giving up what you have given as gifts,
           but of making your face shine
              before the eyes of our brothers.

This we ask of you, Father,
    in the name of your Son Jesus,
        our brother and Lord.

Amen.

A Liturgy for
Lent

I conceive of no particular occasion or frequency for the celebration of this liturgy during the Lenten season. The need of a group to pray together, a need that is born in the spirit, should inspire the liturgy—as frequently or as infrequently as this may be. If, however, it is celebrated regularly, it would be well to alter the form and the readings for the sake of variety.

Father,
we know that you are with us,
   for so you have assured us,
      in your Son, Christ Jesus.
Open our minds and hearts now
   to the transparent light of your Word,
      that we may welcome it in love,
         and that it may illumine the lives we lead.

When you fast, do not put on a gloomy look as the hypocrites do: they pull long faces to let men know they are fasting. I tell you solemnly, they have had their reward. But when you fast, put oil on your head and wash your face, so that no one will know that you are fasting except your Father who sees all that is done in secret; and your Father who sees all that is done in secret will reward you.

Do not store up treasures for yourselves on earth, where moths and woodworms destroy them and thieves can break in and

steal. But store up treasures for yourselves in heaven, where
neither moth nor woodworms destroy them and thieves can-
not break in and steal. For where your treasure is, there will
your heart be also.

(*Mt. 6: 16-21*)

Father, we look forward in these days
to another Easter,
to a renewal of your promise to us.
We are taken up with the bigness of our smallness,
lost in the wonder of another spring,
in the drama of death and rebirth.
Our experience teaches us that birth will always be painful.
How does a man uproot the false pride
which he calls doing your will?
How does he tear up his own lack of concern,
cloaked behind a Church
which he will not trouble to build into a community;
behind a self-sufficient bribery
which masquerades as worship;
behind a love
which costs no more than words?
And always your voice in the still moment,
the call to fall into the ground and die,
to be your seed for our world.

Give us your Spirit, Father, and the strength of love
to shatter the idols we have made.
so busily do we polish our distorted images of you
that we will not recognize you
as you come each day in the flesh:
in homes and in prisons,
in hospitals and in ghettos,
in the loneliness and need of our brothers.

Give us the grace to let you be God,
   rather than the little images we carve.

Father, your Word to us became flesh,
   so that our word might learn to do the same,
   so that love spoken might become love lived
      not only in church, but in your world:
         in office and factory,
         in city and field,
            wherever we find ourselves.

In these days of Lent, Father,
turn our eyes to the fields ripe for harvest.
   We can plow the acre of ourselves so often,
   so delight in turning the soil,
      that nothing,
         not even weeds,
      can grow.
For us, now or never is the hour of your kingdom:
   for the opening of doors and the leveling of walls,
   for laying down fear and taking up the faith
      of the sons of God,
   for planting love and harvesting life.
Move our hearts, we pray,
   through Christ the Lord.

Amen.

A Dinner Liturgy for
Holy Thursday

While not following the ritual in any exacting way, this small celebration has its inspiration in the liturgy of the Hebrew Passover meal: the triple sharing of bread and of the cup, the questions from the children, some of the words of prayer, the awareness of history—all are derived from the traditional seder. *The liturgy as given here might be celebrated as a unit before dinner or, more fittingly, be celebrated in three distinct segments: as grace before the meal, as a prayer just before dessert, and as a final grace at the end of the meal.*

The setting should be plain but festive, with white decor predominating. All that is needed is a plate with two pieces of bread, and a cup for wine. There should also be candles burning on the table and, following the symbolism of the meal, it would be fitting to serve lamb as the main course, if this should prove at all possible.

(*All reach out and touch the dish that holds the bread*)

Blessed are you, Lord our God,
    ruler of the universe!
For you create and give to us
    the fruit of the earth,
        and touch our hearts
            with the holiness of your Word.

79

(*One of the children asks the following question*)

Why do we celebrate this holy meal together?

(*The father breaks one piece of bread in half and lays one half aside; the other half he distributes among all those present*)

This is the bread our fathers in faith
   ate in the desert.
It was the gift of your hands,
   to prepare for yourself a people
     who would love in Spirit and in truth.

(*Eat the bread*)

This is the cup of sacrifice,
   in which your children return to you
     in thanksgiving
       the numberless gifts of your earth.

(*Share the cup*)

Every man of every age, Father,
   you call forth from the Egypt
     of selfishness and sin.
For not only our fathers in faith
   did you lead out of slavery,
     but ourselves with them.

* * *

(*Later in the meal, one of the children asks the following question*)

Why do we break bread tonight,
  and pass around the cup of wine?

(*The father breaks the second piece of bread and distributes
it among all those present*)

This is the bread of the multiplied loaves
    by which the Lord fed
        those who had heard his Word,
            for he would not send them home hungry.
By it they were filled and satisfied,
    and in its strength
        they were nourished for life without end.

(*Eat the bread*)

This is the wine of the promised land
    where the Lord sits at dinner with his children,
    where they join hands around his table
        and lay open their arms and hearts to one another
            in Spirit and in truth.

(*Share the cup*)

***

(*At the end of the meal, one of the children asks the following question*)

What is this bread and wine
    that we share tonight?

(*The father takes the piece of bread that he had laid aside,
and shares it with all those present*)

This is the supper of the Lamb of God
   prepared by our Father from the beginning.
Broken that we might be whole,
   nailed to a cross by his love,
      the Lord Jesus shared himself among men
        that men might live together
          in the peace of God's children.

(*Eat the bread*)

This is the cup of God's blood—
   poured out on the dust of our world
      to make the earth grow green again;
   passed hand to hand among men
      that they might live as children of God.

(*Share the cup*)

Jesus knew that the Father had put everything into his hands, and that he had come from God and was returning to God, and he got up from table, removed his outer garment and, taking a towel, wrapped it around his waist; he then poured water into a basin and began to wash the disciples' feet and to wipe them with the towel he was wearing.

He came to Simon Peter, who said to him, "Lord, are you going to wash my feet?" Jesus answered, "At the moment you do not know what I am doing, but later you will understand." "Never!" said Peter. "You shall never wash my feet." Jesus replied, "If I do not wash you, you can have nothing in common with me." "Then Lord," said Simon Peter," "not only my feet, but my hands and my head as well!" Jesus said, "No one who has taken a bath needs washing; he is clean all over. You too are clean, though not all of you are."

He knew who was going to betray him; that was why he said, "though not all of you are."

When he had washed their feet and put on his clothes again he went back to the table. "Do you understand," he said, "what I have done to you? You call me Master and Lord, and rightly; so I am. If I, then, the Lord and Master, have washed your feet, you should wash each other's feet. I have given you an example so that you may copy what I have done to you."

(*Jn. 13: 3-15*)

Our Father,
on this night when your own Son
   began to freely walk his path to you,
      let us be with you in his Spirit.
Raise to new life our small hearts
   that they may pulse in harmony with his:
      open to all,
      feeling for all,
      prepared to labor in love
         to the end.
And at that end
   may the light of Easter morning
      shine upon us
      and upon all your sons and daughters.
For if you have loved us so much,
   how can we not give ourselves in return?
In your Spirit, Father,
   open our hearts
      with the lance of your love—
         the wound that will never close,
      an invitation for all
         to come in and rest.
(*Join hands, and pray the "Our Father"*)

A Grace for
Independence Day

This, and the graces that follow, are naturally set around the table where the meal will be eaten. They, like sacraments, are not primarily a call for the Lord to bless the food, for everything in our world is already shot through with the holy. They are rather "sacramental" in nature: attempts to make present in celebration the sign-value of things—which is what everything certainly is: a sign pointing to a meaning within, yet beyond, itself. At all graces, I should wish to see those present join hands during the prayer—a further sign of what the shared meal, at its center, is all about.

Our Father, and Father of all men,
    we place ourselves in your presence
        with words of thanksgiving on our lips
            and with deep gratitude in our hearts.
For we celebrate this day
    the grace of freedom
        with which you have blessed our nation,
    and the liberty of spirit
        poured into the hearts of your children
        in Christ Jesus.

Help us to understand, Father,
    that real freedom walks hand in glove
        with living and acting concern;
    that the world of persons and things
        which so livens our spirits
        must be touched only with the hands of a lover.

For neither freedom nor love, Father,
    are ends in themselves,
        but are a share in your power of creation:
            by which the face of our world
                will be made new,
            by which your children will be brought
                to fullness of life in peace.

You have given us this food,
                this home,
                one another,
    only that we may decide
        either to share in the creation of love and unity,
        or to destroy and pass our days in fear.

We thank you, Father, for the good things
    of this world,
        and for the power of choice,
for this is the glory of your own life.
We ask that we may be worthy of it
    in Christ Jesus,
        your Son and our brother.

Amen.

Grace before
Thanksgiving Dinner

To us, your children,
Father,
you have opened your hands
  and have shared with us
    the wonders of your world:
      sun and sky,
      leaf and flower,
      surf and shore.

In your grace,
Father,
you have given us one another.
Into our keeping
  you have placed our selves
  that, united in your love,
  we may mold your earth
    into a home for each and every man:
      where men may live in peace
      and share in the love
        that alone warms life
        and gives it meaning.

For this, all of this
  things both small and great,
  and for the greatness
    caught within the smallest of your creatures,
we thank you.

Father,
despite our best,
our world is still weighted with sorrow:
    your sons and daughters still go hungry;
    your children take up the weapons of Cain
        against their brothers;
    we gouge the face of your world with greed
        and leave a wasteland
           where nothing,
              not even your children,
           may grow.

Keep us thankful, *closing*
Father,
so that we may touch all things,
    and all men,
        only with the delicacy
        of reverence and love.
Keep us aware of the work,
your work,
that you have given into our hands.
For only in your Spirit
    will your kingdom come,
    and that day shine
        when *all* men will see clearly
        that there is indeed reason
           for thanksgiving.

This,
all of this,
we ask in your Spirit,
through our Lord and brother
Christ Jesus.

Amen.

Grace before
Christmas Dinner

Father,
you love men,
  each of them,
and have made your home
  among us.
We offer you today
  our small thanks
    for this food we are about to eat together,
    for the work and love that prepared it,
    for the sparkle and light of this season,
    for our frail efforts at making love come to life
      in our world.
But above all,
we thank you for your Son
  whose coming
  we make present again
    this day.

He came among us in helplessness
  as your Word to man,
  as your way, and truth, and life.
He came as a little Word,
  the only Word we little ones can understand.
He came as a Word quiet and rich with silence,
  as all our best words are.
Your Word to us
  walked with us and talked to us,

88

grew and sweated,
   loved and cried,
   died only to rise,
so that we might know
   that your love for us
   will never be shaken
     despite our worst.

Help us in our thanks
   to bend our strength
     day by day
   toward a Christmas
     yet to come:
   when all men
     of every stock and branch,
     of every color and nation,
       will sit down to table
       and join hands in peace.
This we ask
   through your Son, our brother,
   who comes to us again
     today and all days,
   Christ Jesus the Lord.

Amen.

Grace before
Easter Dinner

The Lord is risen!
Alleluia!
Let us give thanks
and be glad!

Our Father,
Father of all the children of men,
we offer you our thanks this day
for the gift of your Son.
In his rising
he has graced us with the power
of rising above ourselves,
of breaking our hearts of stone,
of walking in the light
that forever brightens in faith
the fear of the shadow of death.

For since the empty tomb,
nothing matters except everything—
and everything is God's.
And this food
which we are about to receive
in the love of your risen Son
is your sign to us
that nothing passes away,
that nothing shall be lost,
but that all shall be changed

90

and touched with newness of life
   in your Spirit.

Keep us ever in your love,
Father,
even as we join hands
  around this table
    in the new richness of life,
    in the hope
      that we, too, shall rise
      into Christ,
    in the faith
      that your Word to us is life,
      and will never be proven false. *Amen*

For this food,
for all things,
for one another,
we thank you *Jesus our Lord*
  in your risen Son. *and we pray in*

Amen. *the words He taught us ....*
    Our Father

The Spirit in Life

A Celebration of
Friendship

*The setting for this celebration might easily be that of a
shared meal, or it might simply be that of a group sitting
together in a living room. In either case, I should wish to see
it marked by whatever expressions of festivity are common
to those participating and with which all feel at home: lighted
candles, flowers, colorful clothing, singing and music, what
have you. While the liturgy does celebrate the present reality
of friendship, it also looks to the future, to the responsibility
of each individual.*

Our Lord Jesus Christ says:
The first commandment is this:
    "Hear, O Israel:
    The Lord our God is one Lord;
    and you shall love the Lord your God
    with all your heart,
    and with all your mind,
    and with all your strength."
The second is like it:
    "You shall love your neighbor as yourself."
There is no other commandment greater than these.
On these two commandments
depend all the law and the prophets.

*There was a lawyer who, to disconcert Jesus, stood up and
said to him, "Master, what must I do to inherit eternal life?"*

He said to him, "What is written in the law? What do you read there?" He replied, "You must love the Lord your God with all your heart, with all your soul, with all your strength, and with all your mind, and your neighbor as yourself." "You have answered right," said Jesus; "do this and life is yours."

But the man was anxious to justify himself and said to Jesus, "And who is my neighbor?" Jesus replied, "A man was once on his way down from Jerusalem to Jericho and fell into the hands of robbers; they took all he had, beat him and then made off, leaving him half dead. Now a priest happened to be traveling down the same road, but when he saw the man, he passed by on the other side. In the same way a Levite who came to the place saw him, and passed by on the other side. But a Samaritan traveler who came upon him was moved with compassion when he saw him. He went up and bandaged his wounds, pouring oil and wine on them. He then lifted him on to his own mount, carried him to the inn and looked after him. Next day, he took out two denarii and handed them to the innkeeper. 'Look after him,' he said, 'and on my way back I will make good any extra expense you have.' Which of these three, do you think, proved himself a neighbor to the man who fell into the robbers' hands?" "The one who took pity on him," he replied. Jesus said to him, "Go, and do the same yourself."

(*Lk. 10: 25-37*)

Blessed are you, Father,
our Father,
    you from whom we came,
    in whose light we walk,
    and to whom we shall return,
that from the very birthday of creation

when your Spirit played over the waters,
you have never ceased to call all your children
   to fellowship with yourself
   and with one another,
in your Son and our brother,
Christ Jesus the Lord.

after petitions

Blessed are you, Father,
for all the works of your hands
   which you have given us.
But most especially
we thank you for one another
   and for this—
      our gathering before you
      in fellowship:
each to each a light
so that our days may not be passed in shadow.
Therefore we are thankful. *and we pray in the words your son taught us; dear Father.*

(*Some appropriate music could be inserted at this point*)

Father, we thank you
for the gift of your Son, *- Son of Mary*
   and for the power of his rising,
      the Spirit that deepens us in love.
Enlighten our understanding
with the intensity of faith; *always*
   that our eyes may be open
      to your abiding life in our midst,
   that our lips may speak peace to all men;
   that the works of our hands and minds
      may awaken all lives to new life
         in Christ.

Amen.

For the time being,
 while we look toward your coming kingdom
  of peace and friendship,
we thank you, too,
that even darkness reminds us of light.
Grant that we, like your Son,
may redeem the time that you have given us.
Kindle our love, Lord,
 as a light for all our brothers,
and let our hands
be your hands for our world—
 touching, blessing, healing:
  a sign in flesh and blood
   of the greater light,
    the fire that you have cast upon the earth.

Only in this way, Father,
in your Spirit,
may we be the true Church of your Son—
 open to all,
  one with all
   in Christ Jesus;
only in this way
can we make our own
the words our Lord taught us.

(*Here the "Our Father" may be recited together*)

For thine is the kingdom and the power
and the glory,
through Jesus Christ,
in the living love of the Holy Spirit,
today and all days
until eternity.

Amen.

On the Visit of Grandparents

With all your heart honor your father,
  never forget the birthpains of your mother.
Remember that you owe your birth to them;
  how can you repay them for what they have done for you?
                                        (Eccl. 7: 27-28)

(One might pause here for a moment of thought; then exchange whatever greetings and signs of affection are customary in the family)

Father, our Father,
you made us in your own image
  and saw that it was not good for us to be alone.
You gave us into one another's keeping,
  and when you found that that was not enough,
    you gave us yourself in the flesh:
      you sent us your own Son.
We indeed, then, have reason to thank you:
  because you have given yourself to us
    as one God in three Persons;
  because the love we live in our days
    is patterned on you:
      love shared,
        the blessing of family life,
          the grace of children.

Now our footsteps must ever follow in yours:
   we never climb alone,
   and our life,
     in all its tenderness and frailty,
   is your life.
Your Word to us took to himself
   life as we live it:
     in togetherness,
        a God who is many,
           and many children who are one.

The flesh we give to one another through our love,
   you have made your flesh.
The living love of parents,
   fountain of children
     and source of their life in body and soul;
the love of parents and children,
   carried on from year to year,
     from generation to generation;
the love of man for his fellow man—
all are touched and brightened by your love,
   which will never rest
     until it has given itself
       to the utmost.

Be on your guard, stay awake, because you never know when the time will come. It is like a man traveling abroad: he has gone from home, and left his servants in charge, each with his own task; and he has told the doorkeeper to stay awake. So stay awake, because you do not know when the master of the house is coming, evening, midnight, cockcrow, dawn; if he

*comes unexpectedly, he must not find you asleep. And what
I say to you I say to all: Stay awake!*

(*Mk. 13: 33-37*)

You, Father, have given us the glory
   of keeping the doors of our hearts and spirits.
In family love,
you have offered to us
   the moments of joy and peace
      that come from leaving that door unlocked.

Our fathers in faith,
   the Scriptures tell us,
opened their doors to strangers
   and often entertained angels unawares,
      entertained those who brought your Word.
But in your goodness,
   you have filled all of us
      with your words of grace.

We thank you, Father,
   because in a special way
      you have trusted us to one another—
         parents and children,
         and grandchildren.
In your grace,
   we have been your hands
      to make one another what we are.
Give us to realize in your Spirit
   that our growth does not cease with age,
      that your Word to us comes in its good time
         and in ways we least expect,

that it comes to us today
  in these hours we give to one another.

Let us pray now together,
  for the sharpness of vision
    that will let us see with clarity
      that we are never finished becoming your children;
      that your work is always to be done,
        your kingdom to be brought to light
          by a love that never sleeps.

(*Join hands and pray the "Our Father"*)

On the Visit of
Relatives

Mindful that the Lord is in our midst,
with hearts alert and open
let us hear his Word:

Anyone who welcomes you welcomes me;
   and those who welcome me welcome the one who sent me.
Anyone who welcomes a prophet because he is a prophet
   will have a prophet's reward;
and anyone who welcomes a holy man
   because he is a holy man
   will have a holy man's reward.
If anyone gives so much as a cup of cold water
   to one of these little ones
      because he is a disciple,
then I tell you solemnly,
   he will most certainly not lose his reward.

(*Mt. 10: 40-42*)

Our Father, and Father of all men,
we join hands before you at this hour
   in peace,
      and we offer you our prayer.

(*Pray the "Our Father"*)

Cleanse our gaze, Father,
   with the light of your love,
      the mother of all true knowledge.
In your care,
   you have offered us a world as your Eucharist
      to be chewed and swallowed by all
         in oneness and peace.
By the ties of flesh,
   you have given us care of one another.
By your grace,
   as we gather here before you,
      the words of rejoicing
         come easily to our lips.

The bonds of family that draw our hearts together
   are the light that you have kindled, Father:
      a light that makes our steps more certain,
         helps us in anxiety,
            and allows us to walk among one another
            without fear.
In the lighted and peopled landscape of our hearts,
   for brief moments full of promise,
      we can say yes to the reality of our lives
        and to your gentle presence.

Unafraid in the thickets and tangles of our minds,
   we can welcome your daybreak without sunset
      when we will see
         that not only this your family
         but *everyone* is a gift of God.
With you at our side, Father,
   you ask us to be your gift to all men:
      but a gift without the giver
         has lost its meaning.
Keep us, Father, close to you.

Everyone moved by the Spirit is a son of God. The spirit you received is not the spirit of slaves bringing fear into your lives again; it is the spirit of sons, and it makes us cry out, "Abba, Father!" The Spirit himself and our spirit bear united witness that we are children of God. And if we are children we are heirs as well: heirs of God and co-heirs with Christ, sharing his sufferings so as to share his glory.

(Rom. 8: 14-17)

All praise be to you, Father,
   all honor be to your Son
      in the love of his Spirit,
         because you have never ceased to visit your people.
Strengthen this family in oneness, Father,
   that this day may be a beginning
      and not an end,
   that your world may be the better
      for the labor of our lives,
   that the affection and peace
      you have sown here through us
         may always grow and blossom.
May it ever spread,
   to your glory
      and to the benefit of your children.

This we ask
   in the name of Christ our brother.

(*Join hands, and pray the "Glory Be to the Father"*)

For Several Families Together

This celebration is intended for an occasion when a somewhat larger than usual group comes together—for the sake of friendship, for serious discussion, for some reason of mutual concern. In this event, I see the unity of the group as of a less intimate quality than that of the family—though this is not to suggest that the bond is any less firm, but rather merely different in kind and in emotional tone. In such a gathering, I would hope that a leader will quite naturally grow out of the assembly, and that he would be accepted in his function without undue effort.

Give thanks to the Lord, for he is good,
his love is everlasting!
Give thanks to the God of gods,
his love is everlasting!
Give thanks to the Lord of lords,
his love is everlasting!
(Ps. 136: 1-3)

The city that closes its gates
   to any man
      is not the city of God.
The heart that locks its door
   to any man
      is not the heart of God.
The community which claims to be satisfied

with its truth,
with its life,
with its love,
   is a community which is dead.
We shall not arrive,
  none of us,
  until we have all arrived,
    each of us,
      in our smallness,
  at our beginning.

*Then if my people who bear my name humble themselves,
and pray and seek my presence and turn from their wicked
ways, I myself will hear from heaven and forgive their sins
and restore their land. Now and for the future my eyes are
open and my ears attentive to the prayer that is offered in
this place. Now and for the future I have chosen and con-
secrated this house for my name to be there forever.*

(2 Chr. 7: 14-16)

(Use the following liturgy if only Christians are present)

Let us join hands and profess our faith:

We believe in God, the Father almighty,
  creator of heaven and earth;
and in Jesus Christ, his only Son, our Lord,
  who was born of the Virgin Mary,
  was crucified, died, and was buried,
  rose from the dead,
  and is now seated at the right hand of the Father;
and in the Holy Spirit,

the holy Catholic Church,
the communion of saints,
the forgiveness of sins,
the resurrection of the body,
and life everlasting.
This is your gift, Father;
we are proud to profess it.

(*Use the following liturgy if non-Christian brothers are present*)

Let us join hands before our Father,
the maker of all things:

Hear, my people: the Lord our God is the one God.
You shall love the Lord your God
with all your heart,
with all your soul,
with all your strength.
Let these words I urge on you today
be written on your heart.
You shall repeat them to your children
and say them to them
whether at rest in your home
or walking abroad,
at your lying down
or at your rising;
you shall fasten them on your head as a sign
and on your forehead as a circlet;
you shall write them on the doorposts of your house
and on your gates. (*Cf. Dt. 6: 4-9*)

(These and similar petitions and responses may be used in the following litany)

That we may never make a lie of your Word by using it
    to justify our own desires . . . *Hear us, Father.*

That fear of our own weakness may never force us
    to close our ears to your call . . .

That concern for our own security may never lead us
    to shut our eyes to the work you have given us . . .

That our own impatience and lack of faith
    may never tempt us to call for signs and wonders . . .

That we may take your Word seriously,
    no matter what it may cost . . .

That we may be open to your unexpected presence
    in the day-by-day routine of our lives . . .

That your presence may be known among us,
    by the strength of our concern for one another . . .

Father of all men,
we come before you in our smallness,
and with the consciousness
    that it is we
        who have set division in your kingdom,
        who have neglected your law of love,
        who have turned our backs upon
           your offer of friendship,

who have so broken your Word
        that it has lost its spirit.
From the dawn of time
when your Spirit played over the waters,
you have never ceased to speak to us
    in ways full of wonder:
        in happiness and pain,
        in peace and in war,
        in the thunders and in the small breezes
            of our souls.
And your Word has always spelled acceptance,
    though each of us differ as do its letters.
Gather us together now, Father,
    to spell your meaning for our world.
Lead us to understand,
    as only you can,
        that nothing which severs us,
            one from another,
                can possibly be your Word to us;
        that this time which we spend together
            is your promise and pledge
                of our life in you.
One with one another,
    as you are one in many.

In Face of
Routine

Our Father,
we confess your presence here among us
   through Christ Jesus, our brother,
      your Word of Love to us.
In fellowship with him,
   each of us becomes your Word,
   each of us takes on a new fullness of meaning
      for every one of your children;
   each of them, in their turn,
      speaks your Word into our world
         and into our hearts.
We thank you.

Father,
we are easily tired:
   the rhythms of the day and of work
      exhaust us,
   and we are only too glad
      for the quiet hours of night and sleep.
So, too, we recall
was you own Son.
Send us, Father,
his creative Spirit,
   the Spirit who will teach us all things,
that your Word for us may remain living,
   and that we may remain living in heart,
      one for another.

At that time Jesus exclaimed, "I bless you, Father, Lord of heaven and of earth, for hiding these things from the learned and the clever and revealing them to mere children. Yes, Father, for that is what it pleased you to do. Everything has been entrusted to me by my Father; and no one knows the Son except the Father, just as no one knows the Father except the Son and those to whom the Son chooses to reveal him.

"Come to me, all you who labor and are overburdened, and I will give you rest. Shoulder my yoke and learn of me, for I am gentle and humble in heart, and you will find rest for your souls. Yes, my yoke is easy and my burden light."

(*Mt. 11: 25-30*)

Father, children fear the darkness,
 but we are disturbed by your light:
  by what it may show us of ourselves,
   as we are, without makeup;
  by the demands it may make upon us:
   a faith that is not a routine,
   a hope that is far from security,
   a love that may cost not less than everything.

Father, children are rarely bored,
 because they ever expect the unexpected
 and discover it in all they do.
Such is your style, Father,
 to meet us where we least look for you,
  so that we may only say with surprise:
   Is *that* what God wants of me?

Share your eyes with us, Father;
   give us the eyes of your Son,
   and teach us that your ways are not our ways.
     Who told us that you are more in the lab
       than in the kitchen?
     Where have we learned that we shall find you
       by reading books, rather than
         by changing or feeding a baby?
     How could we think that prayer is more dear to you
       than living and acting love,
         or that the two could be severed?
     And why are we so blind to you in the sweat
       and worry of work?
We have taught these things to ourselves, Father,
   and would desperately like to think
     that they are your Word to us.

You will come to us, Father,
   where we are,
     or not at all.
And you *do* come,
   because you have never gone;
   because you have created flesh
     and so badly wanted it to know you
       that you embraced flesh yourself.
In your Son,
you have told us that you are,
   and always will be,
flesh;
and that in flesh,
   in persons,
     will you ever remain and be found.

Share with us, Father,

the creative Spirit of your love,
who makes all things new—
for *all* things *are* new:
filled with the strange skill of speech,
and ready to tell us,
your children,
of the wonders of your hands and heart.

In the Absence of
the Father

This liturgy could appropriately be celebrated before a family meal, but a more precise occasion would have to be determined by the needs of the particular family. So, too, the leader of the liturgy would be selected according to the family's preference: perhaps the mother, perhaps one of the older children.

If I flew to the point of sunrise,
or westward across the sea,
your hand would still be guiding me,
your right hand holding me.

If I asked darkness to cover me,
and light to become night around me,
that darkness would not be dark to you;
night would be as light as day.

It was you who created my inmost self,
and put me together in my mother's womb;
for all these mysteries I thank you:
for the wonder of myself, for the wonder of your works.

Lord God, examine me and know my heart,
probe me and know my thoughts;
make sure I do not follow evil ways,
and guide me in the way that is everlasting.

(Ps. 139: 9-14, 23-24)

Father of all men,
we gather before you at this hour
when N., the father of this family, cannot be with us—
with hearts grateful for your love
which makes us ever one.
For since the dawn of your Son's rising,
"good-bye" and "farewell" have lost their meaning,
and only "so long" remains.
Nothing, by your grace, shall ever again be lost.

The father of this family, Lord, is away,
and he has gone in the company of our love;
just as his love and yours have stayed here
with us.
Ebb and flow,
dawn and day,
cloud and sky—
signs that tell of change and movement,
but not of end or separation.

If anyone loves me he will keep my Word,
and my Father will love him,
and we shall come to him
and make our home with him.
Those who do not love me do not keep my words.
And my Word is not my own:
it is the Word of the one who sent me.
I have said these things to you
while still with you;
but the Advocate, the Holy Spirit,
whom the Father will send in my name,
will teach you everything
and remind you of all I have said to you.

Peace I bequeath to you,
my own peace I give you;
a peace the world cannot give, this is my gift to you.
Do not let your hearts be troubled or afraid.
            (*Jn. 14: 23-27*)

Our Father,
though we are slow to understand,
    the stillness of separation, too, is a gift
        from your loving hands.
In the tangle of our days,
    our eyes grow weak and heavy;
        left to themselves,
            the wells of our appreciation soon run dry.
Only when it is taken away
    do we catch sight of the wonder that is ours.
All too easily, we take our father for granted:
    because we are at home
        in the warmth of his arms;
    because we are settled
        by the sounds of his voice;
    because our needs are lulled to rest
        by the fruit of his work.
Now he is removed from our sight and touch,
    so that we may see just how much he is really here:
        for without darkness,
            we would never know the full meaning of light.

While he is away, Father,
    we understand just how great a gift
        we have in him.
We thank you.

(Here break a piece of bread)

Bread broken, Father, remains one;
   your Son's body passed among men remains one;
     all to show us that, in your goodness,
       the love that makes us your family
         has gathered us into oneness forever.

(Here pass the bread around and eat it; either aloud or in private, each member of the family might offer a personal prayer for their father)

Keep our father in your love, Lord,
   and share with him the peace
     which you have promised.
If it is your will,
   bring him home to us soon and safely,
     so that we may live our thanks for him
       to your glory
         in the love of Christ Jesus.

This we ask of you, Father,
   from whom all fatherhood flows,
     in the name of your Son, Jesus our brother,
       and in the power of his Spirit.

Amen.

A Sunday
Liturgy

*This liturgy is intended for use as a family celebration when,
for some reason, the family is unable to participate in the
Sunday Eucharist. With slight adaptation, however, it might
well serve for other and less specific occasions of celebration—
its main thrust being, if you will, a celebration of the "Word
of the world." If possible, I feel that it would be highly
fitting to celebrate this liturgy outdoors.*

Father, and God of all living things,
    maker of our world,
we pause to give you thanks
    because, for eyes instructed by your love,
        your world is a parable without end.
The wonders of leaf and paw,
    the marvel of hands,
        call us to touch in reverence
            and to throw a bridge across loneliness.
And loneliness itself, Lord, is a wonder:
    the return we make
        for being wrapped in the glory of uniqueness,
        for living the life of God
            in your Son, Christ Jesus our brother.

*I am the true vine,
and my Father is the vinedresser.
Every branch in me that bears no fruit
he cuts away,*

and every branch that does bear fruit he prunes
to make it bear even more.
You are pruned already,
by means of the Word that I have spoken to you.
Make your home in me, as I make mine in you.
As a branch cannot bear fruit all by itself,
but must remain part of the vine,
neither can you unless you remain in me.
I am the vine,
you are the branches.
Whoever remains in me, with me in him,
bears fruit in plenty;
for cut off from me you can do nothing.
Anyone who does not remain in me
is like a branch that has been thrown away
—he withers;
these branches are collected and thrown on the fire,
and they are burnt.
If you remain in me
and my words remain in you,
you may ask what you will
and you shall get it.
It is to the glory of my Father
that you should bear much fruit,
and then you will be my disciples.
As the Father has loved me,
so I have loved you.
Remain in my love.

(*Jn. 15: 1-9*)

Father, in your Son
   you have struck roots deep
      into our hearts
         and into the restless give and take of our lives.

In the tabernacle of the world
and in the living temples of your children,
you have kindled the leaping fire of your Spirit
and the soft light of your home.
Unwilling to leave us orphans,
you have gone ahead to prepare a place for us,
even as we today
prepare here a place for you.
The leaf of the vine and the hidden root
may seem far apart;
but, to the eyes of faith, they are ever one:
the vine that seems so still
only that the branches may climb higher.
~~Though we cannot be with our brothers and sisters today,~~
we join ~~them~~ *now* in worship
and give thanks that we are one body:
your body,
in Spirit and in truth,
your family.

(*These or similar petitions and responses may be used in the
following prayer*)

In oneness with all our brothers and sisters,
we offer our prayer to you, ~~Lord~~: *in the words Our
Lord taught us:
Our Father..*

For the members and friends of this family,
that they may ever remain united
in Christ Jesus . . . *Lord, hear our prayer.*

For the Church of God, that, one with Christ,
it may shine as a light of active love
for all peoples . . .

For all Christians, that their eyes may be open
  to the Word of God
      as it comes anew each day . . .

For all men of good will, that their work
  may lead them to peace
    in your kingdom . . .

God saw all he had made, and indeed it was very good.
Evening came and morning came: the sixth day.
God blessed the seventh day and made it holy,
  because on that day he had rested
    after all his work of creating.

                         (Gn. 1: 31; 2: 2-3)

Father,
at the dawn of time you looked with love
  upon our world.
    You saw your traces in the grass of the fields,
    your joy in the dance of the animals,
    your face mirrored in the faces of your children.
And in the fullness of time,
  because man wanted to be more than your child,
you sent your very own Son
  to assure him that your Word was still true,
    that everything is indeed very good.

In our cities and towns,
  you have made your lasting dwelling;
    in factory and in office,
    in classroom and in laboratory,
      your work is still carried on;

in your children's love
is a picture of yourself.
Wherever love is alive
and growing
and working—
there you stand.

Father,
it seems that in these days,
as never before,
you have given us into our own keeping.
Your gift of freedom has put in our grasp
the reins of life and death,
the spring or winter of creation.
Cleanse our gaze, Father,
and keep us from shifting our task onto you:
for not only ourselves,
but also the fate of your Word and your grace,
is our responsibility.

You seem silent, Father,
so that we may be your Word,
so that men will come upon Christ in your world
when they see the effects of our love.
Seem far away and silent, Father,
where we have driven you,
if that is your will for us.
But, as you promised,
share with us your Spirit:
the strength that will keep us
climbing toward you,
the clear vision that will never
lose sight of you,

the working love that will give you
a new home among us.

We ask this today,
in oneness with our brothers and sisters,
through Christ Jesus
and in his Spirit.

Amen.

A Liturgy before
a Family Trip

Remembering now
that we are in the Lord's presence
    and that so we shall be
    no matter where we may travel,
let us pray:

Our Father,
not only have you created all the good things
    of our world,
but you, in your love,
have re-created each of us
    through the gift of your Son.
Through healing what was wounded,
    and straightening what was bent,
you made to happen
an even greater thing:
    after a falling,
        not only a recovery,
            but a creation robed in newness of life.

We ask, Father,
that you enlighten our understanding
    with the intensity and strength of faith,
so that, during these days,
change and novelty may sharpen our vision
    that there is nothing that is not your Word for us.

To expect nothing
is to begin to receive everything.

Awaken each of us, Father,
    to the beauty of your creation:
        of land and sky,
        of seed and leaf,
        of wing and fin,
        of your child, man,
so that we in our turn
    may awaken each of your children
    whom we meet
    to your love
    at the center of the world.
This we ask through Christ Jesus,
our Lord and brother.
Amen.

(*The petitions of the Lord's Prayer may be stated by the
leader, while each of those present may take a turn in praying one of the responses. It would be fitting to pause after
each petition-response for a moment of silent reflection or
for sharing aloud reflections and reactions*)

Our Father in heaven,
hallowed be thy name.

                Father of all,
                your love has led you to the heart of our world,
                and into the pulse of our loves.
                Open our eyes to the new paths
                by which you come to us each day.

Thy kingdom come.

> As we travel, let us help
> to bring your kingdom to each man we meet:
> let us be your Church.

Thy will be done,
in heaven and on earth.

> Father, do your will, and not ours;
> let your day of peace dawn among men.

Give us today
our daily bread.

> Give us bread, Lord, which we need;
> but give us also the gift of seeing
> with the eyes of grace,
> which alone gives meaning to life.

And forgive us our faults,
as we forgive those
who have offended us.

> Give us forgiveness, Lord, for you love us
> not despite our falls,
> but even as we are,
> even as our falls have made us:
> alive, in search of ourselves,
> in search of you.

And lead us not
into temptation.

Lead us where you will, Lord;
provided only that you are with us,
our steps will not be in darkness
and we shall not stumble.

But deliver us from evil,
through Jesus Christ,
our Lord.

Amen.

A Celebration on
Graduation Day

I see this celebration as primarily directed to the family, but they might also desire to have a few close friends take part. Whether the graduate is a son or daughter, the father would appropriately be the leader, but it would also be fitting for a mother to lead this prayer for her own daughter.

There is a season for everything, a time for every occupation under heaven:
A time for giving birth, a time for dying;
a time for planting, a time for uprooting what has been planted.
A time for killing, a time for healing;
a time for knocking down, a time for building.
A time for tears, a time for laughter;
a time for mourning, a time for dancing.
A time for throwing stones away, a time for gathering them up;
a time for embracing, a time to refrain from embracing.
A time for searching, a time for losing;
a time for keeping, a time for throwing away.
A time for tearing, a time for sewing;
a time for keeping silent, a time for speaking.
A time for loving, a time for hating;
a time for war, a time for peace.

(Eccl. 3: 1-8)

What we call an end,
　　the poet tells us,
is often a beginning;
what we are
is the answer that we are giving
　　to the call of a future
　　　　still in the making.
Today, our brother (sister) N. graduates
and receives the human signs of accomplishment
　　and learning,
　　　　the reward of labor
　　　　and the prize of perseverance.

This end, too, is a beginning,
　　the point from which a person
　　　　takes a new step,
and begins to take the measure
　　of the house that is still to be built,
　　of the house that he and all men
　　　　must call home,
　　a home as small as the heart,
　　　　and as wide as a world.

*Jesus said, "Everyone who comes to me and listens to my
words and acts on them—I will show you what he is like.
He is like the man who when he built his house dug, and
dug deep, and laid the foundations on rock; when the river
was in flood it bore down on that house but could not shake
it, it was so well built. But the one who listens and does nothing is like the man who built his house on soil, with no foundations: as soon as the river bore down on it, it collapsed;
and what a ruin that house became!"*

(Lk. 6: 47-49)

Our Father,
we offer you thanks
for the blessing of our intelligence,
for the power of our freedom,
and for the work of love
that you have given into our keeping.

That our minds may be ever open
to the simplicity of wisdom . . . *Hear us, Father.*

That we may always value truth
more than the pride of being right . . .

That we may recognize
that our intelligence is a plain gift
and that we are responsible for its use . . .

That the work of our minds
may always lead toward peace
and brotherhood among all men . . .

That the attraction and power of facts
may never blind us to the heart of the matter . . .

That we may use all your gifts
only to raise up those who are fallen,
and never to make little of your children . . .

That you may grace us with your vision,
and keep us from the refuge of cynicism . . .

Father,
open your eyes and ears
to your Word
    as it comes to us anew each day,
so that we may truly understand
    that, for all its greatness and beauty,
        humanity is not enough.
We celebrate today
both a task accomplished
    and a task still to come:
        the building of the city of God,
        a city of living stones,
        with Christ at its corner.

Send over us the Spirit of your Son,
    the Spirit of light and understanding,
that we may come to the knowledge
    that surpasses all understanding
        and leads all men to peace.
Help us to make our own
the words of your Son,
    so that all men may indeed know
    that we are all brothers,
        all sons of the one Father.

(*Recite together the "Our Father"*)

A Liturgy for a Birthday

This liturgy might easily be set in the party framework in which the actual birthday celebration occurs, though this is hardly of necessity. The idea, however, seems quite appropriate. At any rate, the signs of a birthday celebration in our culture can be integrated with ease into the service of prayer: the cake, the giving of gifts, singing, and what have you. For the very young, whose interest usually gravitates more toward cake and ice cream, the prayer would have to be drastically abbreviated and greatly simplified.

We recall, my children (my brothers and sisters, etc.),
that where two or three are gathered
   in the name of Jesus,
there the Lord makes his home
   in their midst.
We return his love,
   and make our home,
   build our home,
   in him.
Today we rejoice in the mystery
   that has been shared with us:
   time and change.
Years slip by,
   as children grow into men and women,
   as men and women flower into fathers and mothers,
   into grandfathers and grandmothers.

But always love remains—
   firm and unshifting,
   giving,
   singing in the storms,
   growing and changing,
   yet ever abiding.

At that time, Jesus said to Nicodemus:
"I tell you most solemnly,
unless a man is born from above,
he cannot see the kingdom of God."
Nicodemus said, "How can a grown man be born?
Can he go back into his mother's womb
and be born again?"
Jesus replied:
"I tell you most solemnly,
unless a man is born through water and the Spirit,
he cannot enter the kingdom of God:
what is born of the flesh is flesh;
what is born of the Spirit is spirit.
Do not be surprised when I say:
You must be born from above.
The wind blows wherever it pleases;
you hear its sound,
but you cannot tell where it comes from
or where it is going.
That is how it is with all who are born of the Spirit."

                                             (Jn. 3: 3-8)

Our Father,
Father of all things,

keep alive in us
   through the spiral of our years
   the life of the child,
      the Spirit of love,
      whom you have brought to birth
      in us.

Open our eyes and all our senses
   with the brightness of love
      that we may catch sight of your light
         in the play of the small lights
            that we kindle;
      that we may ever hear your call
         in the voices of those your children
            to whom others close their ears;
      that we may enjoy without greed
         the sweet and pleasing tastes of your world;
      that our hands may be free and open in giving
         rather than clenched in anger and hatred.
For unless we are born ever anew
   as little children,
we cannot live a fully human life
   in fellowship with you.

We thank you for your gift of time,
   for the past year *season*
   that we celebrate:
      time in which to grow ourselves
         and to plant in those days
         the flowers of tomorrow;
      time in which to harvest love and its memories—
         the shared dreams,
         and sorrows,
         failings and disappointments,

smiles and touches,
   that make us what we are,
      your children,
   and give promise of what we shall be.

And today,
we thank you simply for this day
   together:
      for sweetness and light,

(Light the cake)

   for song and the music of voices,
   and for the sharing of gifts,
      in which we share ourselves.

(Sing "Happy Birthday")

Our wishes are shortsighted.
   We wish for the good things of your earth,
     each of us,
     as we must.
   But we wish most of all
     that you keep us,
     each of us,
     all of us,
     every one of your children,
  in your love
     and in your peace.

(Blow out the candles and give gifts)

On the Anniversary of Marriage

A liturgy to be celebrated either within the family or with other friends and relatives invited. Certainly a "public" quality would be in keeping with the renewal of the promises of marriage. The setting is around a table with candles and flowers, the wedding ring(s) on a small plate at the center.

The Lord God said, "It is not good that the man should be alone. I will make him a helpmate." So from the soil the Lord God fashioned all the wild beasts and all the birds of heaven. These he brought to the man to see what he would call them; each one was to bear the name the man would give it. The man gave names to all the cattle, to all the birds of heaven and all the wild beasts. But no helpmate suitable for man was found for him. So the Lord God made the man fall into a deep sleep. And while he slept, he took one of his ribs and enclosed it in flesh. The Lord God built the rib he had taken from the man into a woman, and brought her to the man. The man exclaimed:

> *"This at last is bone from my bones,*
> *and flesh from my flesh!*
> *This is to be called woman,*
> *for this was taken from man."*

137

This is why a man leaves his father and mother and joins himself to his wife, and they become one body.

(*Gn. 2: 18-24*)

Our Father,
   you in whose sight we live and love,
we come before you—
   husband and wife (and children) (*mention names*)—
     our life on earth
      the image of your eternal giving of yourself.
For the past year,
   in the day-to-day pulse of our life together,
you have placed at our fingertips
   the materials from which we are to build
     our life in you:
       laughter and smiles,
       tears and frowns,
       success and failure—
       the ebb and flow of affection.
For this is what your Word is all about:
   the life your Son lived among us
     once more lived fully with each new day.

Husbands should love their wives just as Christ loved the Church and sacrificed himself for her to make her holy. He made her clean by washing her in water with a form of words, so that when he took her to himself she would be glorious, with no speck or wrinkle or anything like that, but holy and faultless. In the same way, husbands must love their wives as they love their own bodies; for a man to love his wife is for him to love himself. A man never hates his own body, but he feeds it and looks after it; and that is the way Christ treats the Church, because it is his body—and we are its living parts. For this reason, a man must leave his father and mother and be joined to his wife, and the two will become one body. This mystery has many implications; but I am saying it applies to Christ and the Church. To sum up: you too, each one of you, must love his wife as he loves himself; and let every wife respect her husband.

(Eph. 5: 25-33)

EXCHANGE OF RING(S)

(The following, or something similar, to be said by the husband)

N. *(name of wife)*,
n. *(number of years)* years ago
   I circled your finger with this ring
      as a sign of unbroken love
      and as a promise of care and concern
         without end.
Today, I repeat that promise
   and take you again to myself
      as God's gift.

(Place the ring on her finger)

We are one body and one life in Christ,
   come what may,
      now and forever.

(The following, or something similar, to be said by the wife)

N. (*name of husband*),
n. (*number of years*) years ago,
   I accepted a ring from you,
      a sign of my willingness
         to live within the circle of your love.
Today, I repeat that promise
   and take you to myself
      as God's gift.
And in my turn,
   I give you this ring
      as a sign of my faithfulness
      and as a promise of my love.

(*Place the ring on his finger*)

We are one body and one life in Christ,
   come what may,
      now and forever.

Father, from whom all love comes,
   and in whom all love flourishes,
      we give you thanks for our years
         of growth together.
Send over us your Spirit,
   so that day by day
      we may lay our hearts open to one another,
        and in one another to you.
Firm us in your love,
   that our arms may be wide
     not only for one another
       but for all your children—
         especially those who most need us.
May the circle of our wedding bands spread,

ever wider and ever stronger,
    until it gathers all men into your love.
For you are our Father,
  and we are your children
    in Christ Jesus the Lord.

(*Pray the "Our Father," and exchange kisses*)

New Beginnings

A Liturgy at the Deathbed

Death, I think, must be a moment of crisis, a moment in which the personal energies of an individual are uniquely activated and gathered into concentration. It is the moment of life. At the same time, this moment gives birth to intense activity for those who stand by: emotions, questions, doubts, and all the intricate and fragile movements of love. In face of the last question, I feel that we can only voice once more the questions and answers of Scripture; thus this liturgy grows almost as a dialogue. The prayer may be paced slowly or quickly and may be distributed among as many readers as seems fitting. Pauses for personal thought will, I hope, emerge quite naturally. Only the situation and a judgment of what is best for the dying person can determine whether the liturgy should actually be celebrated in his or her presence. The family and friends might use it for their own prayerful meditation in another room—in the parlor, for example.

My brothers and sisters,
we recall that we are in the presence
   of him who is,
in the presence of him who is Love itself.
In him we live
   and move
   and have our very being.
Into his love
we give his child,

our brother (sister) N. (*name of the dying person*),
   with sorrow at parting,
   but with joy in victory.

What is man, what purpose does he serve?
   What is the good in him, and what the bad?
Take the number of a man's days;
   a hundred years is very long.
Like a drop of water from the sea, or a grain of sand,
   such are these few years compared with eternity.

                                             (Sir. 18, 8-10)

> *I tell you, most solemnly,*
> *unless a wheat grain falls on the ground and dies*
> *it remains only a single grain;*
> *but if it dies,*
> *it yields a rich harvest.* (Jn. 12: 24-25)

> *Whoever listens to my words,*
> *and believes in the one who sent me,*
> *has eternal life;*
> *without being brought to judgment*
> *he has passed from death to life.* (Jn. 5: 24)

Is not man's life on earth
   nothing more than forced service,
his time no better than hired labor? (Jb. 7: 1)

> *I think that what we suffer in this life can never be compared to the glory, as yet unrevealed, which is waiting for us. From the beginning till now the entire creation, as we know, has been groaning in one great act of giving birth; and*

*not only creation, but all of us who possess the
first-fruits of the Spirit, we too groan inwardly
as we wait for our bodies to be set free. For I am
certain of this: neither death nor life, no angel,
no prince, nothing that exists, nothing still to
come, not any power, or height or depth, nor any
created thing, can ever come between us and the
love of God made visible in Christ Jesus our Lord.*
(*Rom.* 8: 18, 22-23, 38-39)

Who told you that you were naked? (*Gn.* 3: 11)

*Naked I came from my mother's womb,
naked I shall return.
The Lord gave, the Lord has taken back.
Blessed be the name of the Lord.* (*Jb.* 1: 21)

*Indeed, I know it is as you say:
How can man be in the right in the face of God?* (*Jb.* 9: 1)

*Yet you are merciful to all, because you can do
all things
and overlook men's sins so that they can repent.
Yes, you love all that exists, you hold nothing of
what you have made in abhorrence,
for had you hated anything, you would not have
formed it.
And how, had you not willed it, could a thing per-
sist,
how be conserved if not called forth by you?
You spare all things because all things are yours,
Lord, lover of life,
you whose imperishable Spirit is in all.
Little by little, therefore, you correct those who
offend,*

> you admonish and remind them of how they have
>   sinned,
> so that they may abstain from evil and trust in
>   you, Lord. (*Wis. 11: 21—12: 2*)

Can any power be found within myself,
has not all help deserted me? (*Jb. 6: 13*)

> Do not be afraid, for I have redeemed you; I have
>   called you by your name, you are mine.
> Should you pass through the sea, I will be with
>   you;
> or through rivers, they will not swallow you up.
> Should you walk through fire, you will not be
>   scorched
> and the flames will not burn you.
> Do not be afraid, for I am with you.
>
> > (*Is. 43: 1-2, 5*)

How far from saving me are the words I groan!
I call all day, my God, but you never answer,
all night long I call and cannot rest. (*Ps. 22: 1-2*)

> I myself will pasture my sheep, I myself will show
> them where to rest—it is the Lord God who
> speaks. I shall look for the lost one, bring back
> the stray, bandage the wounded and make the
> weak strong. I shall watch over the healthy. I shall
> be a true shepherd to them. (*Ez. 34: 15-16*)

> The sheep that belong to me listen to my voice;
> I know them and they follow me.
> I give them eternal life;

they will never be lost
and no one will ever steal them from me.
(*Jn.* 10: 27-28)

I have shown my love for you, says the Lord God.
But you ask, "How have you shown your love?" (*Mal.* 1: 2)

A man can have no greater love
than to lay down his life for his friends.
(*Jn.* 15: 13)

Indeed, I promise you,
today you will be with me in paradise.
(*Lk.* 23: 43)

But you, who do you say that I am? (*Mt.* 16: 16)

He is God, not of the dead, but of the living; for
to him all men are in fact alive. (*Lk.* 21: 38)

I am the resurrection and the life.
If anyone believes in me, even though he dies he
will live,
and whoever lives and believes in me
will never die. (*Jn.* 11: 25-26)

Why are you so frightened,
you men of little faith? (*Mt.* 8: 26)

For the mountains may depart,
the hills be shaken,
but my love for you will never leave you

*and my covenant of peace with you will never be
   shaken,*
says the Lord God who takes pity on you.

                        (Is. 54: 10)

Why are you weeping?
Whom are you looking for? (Jn. 20: 15)

You will be sorrowful,
but your sorrow will turn to joy.
A woman in childbirth suffers,
because her time has come;
but when she has given birth to the child she for-
   gets the suffering
in her joy that a man has been born into the
   world.
So it is with you: you are sad now,
but I shall see you again, and your hearts will be
   full of joy,
and that joy no one shall take from you.

                        (Jn. 16: 20-22)

May the Lord bless you and keep you.
May the Lord let his face shine on you
   and be gracious to you.
May the Lord uncover his face to you
   and bring you peace. (Nm. 6: 24-26)

May the Lord keep you in his love
as we keep you in ours,
forevermore and evermore.

Amen.

For a Death
within the Family

The precise time and circumstances for the celebration of this liturgy—whether before or after the burial, how long before or after, whether other relatives besides immediate family should be present—must rest completely with those concerned. Suffice it to say that the liturgy is not designed to rake emotional coals into flame, but rather to encourage a sense of Christian serenity and peace.

Though the liturgy could be conducted before a family meal, this is not of necessity—so long as the celebration is not forced, it might take place at whatever time the family might normally be together. It is the feelings of the family that should spark the call for the celebration and an unfeeling regimentation should be avoided at all costs.

The Lord God is my shepherd,
   I lack nothing.
In meadows of green grass he lets me lie.
To the waters of repose he leads me;
   there he revives my soul.

He guides me by paths of virtue
   for the sake of his name.

Through I pass through a gloomy valley,
   I fear no harm;

beside me your rod and your staff
  are there, to hearten me.

You prepare a table before me
  under the eyes of my enemies;
you anoint my head with oil,
  my cup brims over.

Ah, how goodness and kindness pursue me,
  every day of my life;
my home, the house of the Lord God,
  as long as I live!

                              (*Ps. 23*)

Our Father, God of all the living,
we come before you questioning and uncertain,
    because, in your good time,
        the father (mother, child, etc.) of this family
        N. (*mention name of deceased*)
            has passed into your hands.
We have died this death of the one we love,
    and part of our hearts has gone with him (her).
And though we walk hand-in-hand with death
    all our days, Father,
        we are still awed and deeply stirred
            by this consecration
                in the Eucharist of his (her) life.

Everything that is flesh is not the same flesh: there is hu-
man flesh, animals' flesh, the flesh of birds and the flesh of
fish. Then there are heavenly bodies and there are earthly
bodies; but the heavenly bodies have a beauty of their own

and the earthly bodies a different one. The sun has its bright-
ness, the moon a different brightness, and the stars a differ-
ent brightness, and the stars differ from one another in bright-
ness. It is the same with the resurrection of the dead: the
thing that is sown is perishable but what is raised is imper-
ishable; the thing that is sown is contemptible but what is
raised is glorious; the thing that is sown is weak but what is
raised is powerful; when it is sown it embodies the soul, when
it is raised it embodies the spirit.

(*1 Cor. 15: 39-44*)

Our Father, we offer you our prayer
   in the name of your own Son,
      who shed tears at the death of his friend Lazarus,
      who passed the doors of death himself
         and handed his spirit into your keeping.
The horizon of our sight is limited,
   but the vision of our belief reaches far beyond.
For in the empty grave of your own Son
   you have given us to know
      that death and darkness have not the last word:
         the seed becomes fruit;
         the caterpillar spreads wings;
         and from the stillness of the earth
            rises the glory of your new life.   *Amen*

To share his spirit with us, Father,
   your Son had to take leave of us;
our father (mother, etc.) N. (*name of deceased*)
   has found life in you
      only to share it with us
         by touching us with a love
            more tender and closer than any we have yet known.

He (she) shines brightly in our hearts,
　　for well we know
　　　　that only that dies
　　　　which we allow to die.

Our Father and living God,
bless N. (*name of deceased*) with life without measure—
　　life ever close to us
　　　　in you.
This we ask in the name of your living Son,
　　Christ Jesus.

(*Join hands*)

Give everlasting rest to him (her), Lord,
　　and let your light shine upon him (her).
May he (she) rest in your peace,
　　and in our love.

Amen!

On the Death
of a Friend

The liturgy is conceived as taking place around a table, with a single candle burning and the rest of the lights in the room extinguished. In the center of the table, a piece of bread.

Nothing therefore can come between us and the love of Christ, even if we are troubled or worried, or being persecuted, or lacking food or clothes, or being threatened or even attacked. As Scripture promised: For your sake we are being massacred daily, and reckoned as sheep for the slaughter. These are the trials through which we triumph, by the power of him who loved us.

For I am certain of this: neither death nor life, no angel, no prince, nothing that exists, nothing still to come, not any power, or height or depth, nor any created thing, can ever come between us and the love of God made visible in Christ Jesus our Lord.

(Rom. 8: 35-39)

You are rightly to be praised, Father
   and with reason is your name blessed
      today and all days.
For you have called us out of darkness
   into the light of your world

and given us promise of endless summer
and new life in your kingdom.

(Turn on the other lights)

Do not let your hearts be troubled.
Trust in God still, and trust in me.
There are many rooms in my Father's house;
if there were not, I should have told you.
I am going now to prepare a place for you,
and after I have gone and prepared you a place,
I shall return to take you with me;
so that where I am
you may be too.
You know the way to the place where I am going.
$\qquad$ *(Jn. 14: 1-4)*

Father, we have certainly been blessed
    in your gift of N. *(name of deceased)*,
        with whom we shared bread,
        who joined hands with us around our table,
        who carried the joy of himself (herself)
            into our home and into our hearts.
We shall miss him (her),
    though the hurt we carry
        is your very assurance
            that he (she) is still close to us.

(Here break the bread)

Our Father,
we break bread once again,
    remembering that night

when your Son passed through pain
into your loving hands.
Share with us the strength
to trust your eyes rather than our own:
he was broken and crushed,
but you filled him with a glory
that splintered the doors
.with which his friends had locked their hearts;
he seemed cold in the grave,
but the warmth of his spring
cracked the ice around men's souls.
he returned to you,
but his Spirit is undying fire
upon our earth.

(*Pass bread around*)

And this bread speaks to us also, Father,
of all who live in him,
of N. (*name of deceased*), our brother (sister),
as we take it to ourselves in oneness.
What seems unliving
is charged with the life of your Son;
what seems to pass away,
is made flesh of our flesh,
bone of our bone.

(*Eat the bread together*)

By your grace, Father,
we believe that N. (*name of deceased*)
is at rest in you,
is part of us as is this bread.
Share his (her) joy and peace with us

as we share food together,
and keep unbroken to the end
the circle of affection
begun at your table.

This we ask of you, Father,
in Christ Jesus.

(*Join hands, and pray together the "Gloria"*)

On the Anniversary
of Death

This liturgy might take place with the group sitting around the table on which is burning a single candle surrounded by flowers. The leader might be a relative of the deceased person, or whoever within the family has been and is especially attached to him or to her.

In the peace of Christ . . . *Let us pray to the Lord!*

In confidence and hope . . .

In the promise and power of love . . .

In the strength of the Spirit . . .

For one another . . .

For all men of good will . . .

For all our brothers and sisters
   who have gone before us in the Lord . . .

For N. (*name of deceased*)
   who has come to fullness of life
   in the hands of the one whom we call Father . . .

I will tell you something that has been secret: that we are not all going to die, but we shall all be changed. This will be instantaneous, in the twinkling of an eye, when the last trumpet sounds. It will sound, and the dead will be raised, imperishable, and we shall be changed as well, because our present perishable nature must put on imperishability and this mortal nature must put on immortality.

When this perishable nature has put on imperishability, and when this mortal nature has put on immortality, then the words of Scripture will come true: "Death is swallowed up in victory. Death, where is your victory? Death, where is your sting?" Now the sting of death is sin, and sin gets its power from the law. So let us thank God for giving us the victory through our Lord Jesus Christ.

(1 Cor. 15: 51-57)

Our Father,
we come to you in joy
   for your favor of unending life
      made known in Christ Jesus.
In him, all persons and all things are filled with spirit
   and poured out over our world.
The love of N. (*name of deceased*)
   which was a sun to our small circle
      can now begin to spread its warmth
         far and wide—
            a miracle beyond our grasp,
            a glory past our dreaming.

I tell you most solemnly,
if you do not eat the flesh of the Son of Man
and drink his blood,

you will not have life in you.
Anyone who does eat my flesh and drink my blood
has eternal life,
and I shall raise him up on the last day.
For my flesh is real food
and my blood is real drink.
He who eats my flesh and drinks my blood
lives in me
and I live in him.
As I, who am sent by the living Father,
myself draw life from the Father,
so whoever eats me will draw life from me.
This is the bread come down from heaven;
not like the bread our ancestors ate:
they are dead,
but anyone who eats this bread will live forever.

(*Jn. 6: 53-58*)

Our Father,
during his (her) years on earth,
   we were often refreshed by the spirit
      of your son (daughter) N. (*name of deceased*).
And all too frequently,
   our eyes were not quick enough
      to catch your fragile movements
         in the sacrament of his (her) life.
His (her) return home n. (*insert correct number*) years ago
   was in the time you saw of his (her) fullness,
   in the season of his (her) ripeness for your kingdom.
The caterpillar, at your Word, Father,
   will spread the wings of the butterfly—
      your sons and daughters will come home to you,

however much our own needs
would like to hold them back.

And now, Father, we meet in joy
at our brother's (sister's) victory:
for even our oneness in prayer
tells us that nothing has been lost,
but all changed,
and wrapped in newness of life.
N. (*name of deceased*) is still among us,
living and caring for us in his (her) love.
He (she) is grace for us,
carrying our own love into your heart, Father,
and your heart into our love
today and tomorrow.

Rain upon us your spirit, Father,
that our growth in your world
may ready us for still another and even happier meeting
in days to come.
This we ask
in the name and power of your Son,
risen and living,
today and all days.

(*Join hands and pray the "Our Father"*)

The Beginning
and the End

The Institution of
the Eucharist

(Many of the prayers of celebration in the foregoing liturgies could be expanded for use in a bread and wine Eucharist by the inclusion of a eucharistic institution account, of which the following is offered as a simple model)

On the night when he was betrayed
    by the kiss of one closest to him,
he sat down to dinner with his friends.
Taking bread into his hands,
    he gave you thanks, blessing it.

(Here break the bread)

He broke the bread
    and gave it to them with the words:

    This is my body which is broken for you.

    This bread which is broken
    is the sign of his making:
    as bread are we to be broken,
        one for another.

At the end of dinner,
    he took a cup of wine, gave you thanks,
    and passed it to them with the words:

This is the cup of my blood,
the cup of the new covenant.
This blood is shed for you
   and for all men.
so that sins may be forgiven.

This cup which is one
is the sign of his making:
only crushed as grapes,
   one for another,
can we live in him.